Ellery Bicknell Crane

The ancestry of Edward Rawson, Secretary of the Colony of Massachusetts Bay:

With some account of his life in old and New England.

Ellery Bicknell Crane

The ancestry of Edward Rawson, Secretary of the Colony of Massachusetts Bay:
With some account of his life in old and New England.

ISBN/EAN: 9783337733636

Printed in Europe, USA, Canada, Australia, Japan

Cover: Foto ©ninafisch / pixelio.de

More available books at **www.hansebooks.com**

The Ancestry of Edward Rawson,

SECRETARY

of the

Colony of Massachusetts Bay.

WITH SOME ACCOUNT OF HIS LIFE IN OLD AND

NEW ENGLAND.

BY

ELLERY BICKNELL CRANE,

Compiler of the Revised Memoir of Edward Rawson, with Genealogical
Notices of his Descendants, published in 1875.

WORCESTER, MASS.:

PRIVATE PRESS OF FRANKLIN P. RICE.

1887.

CONTENTS.

.

PORTRAIT OF EDWARD RAWSON   Frontispiece

RAWSON FAMILY COAT OF ARMS   1

ANCESTRY OF EDWARD RAWSON   3

CHILDREN OF EDWARD RAWSON   22

WILL OF THE GRANDFATHER OF EDWARD RAWSON   27

WILL OF THE FATHER OF EDWARD RAWSON   28

RAWSON AND STANHOPE PEDIGREE   31

RAWSON PEDIGREE CONTINUED   32, 33, 38

ADDENDA   34

STANHOPES CONNECTED WITH THE RAWSONS   39

STANHOPE PEDIGREE   46 to 49

SIR JOHN RAWSON   50

Edward Rawson.

Ancestry of Edward Rawson.

It has ever been a source of pride among our forefathers to be able to trace their lineage to a noble ancestry. Although in this, the nineteenth century, we find not so much stress attached to noble birth as formerly, yet there appears no good reason why it should not be cited and used as an incentive to more worthy living and superior attainments. At the time of the publication of the Revised Rawson Family Memorial, in the year 1875, comparatively little was known concerning the ancestry of Edward Rawson, who was for so many years Secretary of the Massachusetts Bay Colony. Soon after the volume referred to had found its way into the hands of the public, the writer chanced to be strolling among the monuments of the departed dead in the old church yard, at Mendon, Mass.; and while examining a slab of slate-stone that once formed the end of a cromlech over the grave where had been deposited the remains of a son and daughter of Capt. William Rawson, grandson of the Secretary, a figure was discovered, which, on removing the lichen, proved to be that of a family armorial. Of this a drawing was carefully made, and steps immediately taken toward finding the name of its original owner.

A brief research revealed the fact that the armorial was one borne by Sir John Rawson, Knight of Rhodes, and of St. John of Jerusalem.* He was elected Prior of Kilmainham in 1511,† and in 1517, by order of King Henry VIII., was sworn Privy Councillor of Ireland, and Lord Treasurer of that Kingdom. In 1526, at

---

* The Order of St. John began in the year 1120. They wore long gowns or robes of black, with white crosses upon the breast.

† The Priory of Kilmainham was situated near Dublin.

the request of King Henry VIII., he was appointed by the grand master, Turcopolier of the order of Knights of St. John. This office he exchanged with Sir. John Babington for the dignity of Prior of Ireland.

In the 33d year of Henry VIII. (1542), Sir John surrendered the Priory of Kilmainham to the King, obtaining therefor a pension of 500 marks out of the estate of the Hospital, and as he had sat in the Irish House of Lords, as Prior of Kilmainham, he exchanged his spiritual dignity for a temporal peerage, being created Viscount Clontarff. This title became extinct at his death in the year 1560. He left a daughter, Catherine, who married Rowland Whyte, son of Patrick Whyte, second Baron of the Exchequer in Ireland. This armorial of Sir John Rawson was placed in one of the windows of Swingfield church, a chapel dedicated to St. Peter. The Parish of Swingfield was included in the property of the Knights of St. John of Jerusalem, and is located five miles north from Folkestone, in the County of Kent.

Sir John Rawson had four brothers and three sisters. Avery and Christopher were citizens and merchants of London, dealers in the staple of Calais. Christopher owned Old Wool Quay, in Petty Wales (Lower Thomas Street), having received it by his mother's will. He died in 1518, and was buried at Allhallow's Barking, Great Tower Street.

Richard bore the title of Doctor of Divinity as well as Doctor of Laws; was Prebendary of Durnsford, in Salisbury; Archdeacon of Essex, 1502; Rector of St. Olaves, Hart Street, 1510; Canon of Windsor, 1521; was Vicar of the church at Beaconsfield, Buckinghamshire, having been presented there July 25, 1525. He rebuilt the Parsonage House, where his arms were remaining in 1728. Died in 1543.

The other brother, Nicholas, became master of the Free Chapel at Gressenhall, County of Norfolk. Died leaving two sons, John and Walter.

The elder brother, Avery, aside from being a merchant in London, was styled of Aveley, a Parish fourteen or fifteen miles east of London, in the County of Essex. His son, Nicholas

Rawson, was not only an owner of an estate in Aveley, but also held lands there in fee simple by copy of Court Roll. He married the widow of William Copley, Esq., whose maiden name was Beatrix Cooke, daughter of Sir Philip Cooke, Knight of Giddea Hall, County of Essex. She died at the home of her daughter, Lady Anne Rawson Stanhope, at Shelford, January 14, 1554. Nicholas Rawson died in 1529, leaving four children; a daughter Anne became the wife of Sir Michael Stanhope, Knight of Shelford, County of Nottingham. Sir Michael seems to have been held in high favor by King Henry VIII., for on the 24th of Nov. 1538, he, by letters patent, granted to him and his wife Anne, the house and site of the Priory, and Almshouses, etc., within the Parish of Shelford, including 164 acres of land with all the appurtenances. February 5, 1540, he bestowed upon him the Manor of Shelford, and the Rectories of the parish churches of Shelford, Sarendale, Gedling, Burton Jorz, Forth-Ruskham, and all manors, messuages, lands, tenants, etc., in Shelford, Sarendale, Newton, Brigford, Gunthorpe, Lowdham, Cathorpe, Horingham, Bulcote, Gedling, Carlton, Stoke, Lamcote, Flintham, Long-Collingham, Cawnton, the town of Nott, Newark, Burton Jorz, and Forth-Ruskham, all in the county of Nottingham, and late belonging to the monastery of Shelford, Michael Stanhope, Esq., paying therefor 119*l* per annum.

In the year 1544 the King appointed him Steward over the Lordships of Holderness and Cottingham. In 1546 he was dubbed a Knight at Hampton Court, and in the following year received the appointment of Governor of Hull. In 1548 he was chosen Chief Gentleman of the Privy Chamber to King Edward VI. The high and responsible position to which he had now attained, brought with it grave results. The rivalry and jealousy that existed among those who held high places among the King's Councillors, made it extremely hazardous in those days to occupy exalted positions, especially as taking the life of a person who stood in the way of the promotion of another, seems to have been comparatively easily arranged for, on the ground that the success or wellbeing of the Government demanded it. Thus the flattering career of our noble Knight was soon to reach a close.

Sir Edward Stanhope, the father of Sir Michael, was twice married. The name of his first wife was Adelina, daughter of Sir Gervas Clefton, by whom he had Richard and Michael. After the death of Michael's mother, he married Elizabeth, daughter of Fulc Bourchier, Lord Fitz Warin, by whom he had a daughter Anne, who became the wife of Edward Seymour, Duke of Somerset, who was uncle as well as Protector to King Edward VI. Through the belief that his brother Thomas (Lord Seymour,) had been intriguing against him, the Protector had him arrested, tried for treason, condemned, and beheaded on the 20th of March, 1549. But soon the tables were turned. A powerful rival to the Duke of Somerset appeared in the person of John Dudley, Earl of Warwick and Duke of Northumberland, who had been compelled to resign the office of Lord High Admiral by the Protector, in order that his brother, Thomas Seymour, might receive that appointment, and was only waiting for an opportunity to get his revenge. Dudley had again been made Lord High Admiral, and soon succeeded in gaining extensive influence among the Lords of the Council, and was in especial favor with the King. So skillful was he in conducting his efforts that he finally succeeded in influencing the King to sign the deposition of his Uncle the Protector, and on the 14th of October, 1551, he, with the Duchess and several other persons, quite likely Sir Michael Stanhope among the number, were sent as prisoners to the Tower. On it appearing that the life of the Duke of Northumberland was in danger, the King allowed the law to take its course. The Protector and his brother-in-law, Sir Michael Stanhope were tried and condemned to death, the Duke of Somerset being beheaded on Friday, the 22d day of January, 1552, Sir Michael sharing the same fate on the 26th day of the month following. That the latter may have been made a confidant of, and was under obligations to follow the instructions and dictates of his superior, the Duke of Somerset, is all we would offer in extenuation of the crime for which he was made to suffer the penalty of death.

Anne Rawson, the widow of Sir Michael Stanhope, was born about the year 1512, and as a fitting testimonial to her as a mother, we can say that notwithstanding the early and tragic death of her husband, she, with true womanly courage, devoted her life to the welfare of her children, and their success in after years shows with what faithfulness and good judgment that care was bestowed. Out of eleven children, three, Margaret, William and Edward died in infancy. Thomas, the eldest, was Knighted at Kenilworth in the year 1575. He married Margaret, daughter of Sir John Port, by whom he had Sir John, who was the father of Philip Stanhope, first Earl of Chesterfield.

Edward, the second son, became one of the Queen's Council in the north of England, and died in 1608. The third son was Sir John Stanhope of Harrington, gentleman to the Privy Chamber to Queen Elizabeth, and created Lord Stanhope of Harrington in the year 1605. Edward, the fourth son, became a Doctor of Civil Law, and Master in Chancery. The fifth son, Sir Michael Stanhope of Sudbourn, County of Suffolk, Knighted by King James, May 7th, 1603, was gentleman of the Privy Chamber to Queen Elizabeth. The sixth, a daughter, Eleanor, married Thomas Cooper, Esq. Seventh, Julian, married John Hotham, Esq. Eighth, Jane, married Sir Roger Townsend.

The eminent and responsible positions in State and Council to which the children of Lady Anne Rawson Stanhope were called and retained, furnishes a lasting tribute to the memory of a faithful and devoted mother.

Lady Stanhope survived the death of her husband nearly thirty-five years, six days only wanting to complete that time. She died on the 20th of February, 1587, at the old home in Shelford, where she was buried.

The old house at Shelford, was garrisoned for King Charles I., during the Civil wars, and one Philip Stanhope was in command and lost his life during an assault made by the enemy Oct. 27, 1645, when the place was captured and the house burned to the ground.

As the fruit of the marriage of Sir Michael Stanhope and Anne Rawson, we have had, during the years that have intervened, many prominent and illustrious personages whose lives have adorned the pages of English history. Notably among them are the Earls of Chesterfield, of Harrington and of Stanhope.

The merchant, Christopher Rawson, brother of Sir John, and the owner of the Old Wool Quay in London, was twice married. First to Margaret ——, afterward to Agnes, daughter of William Burke. By the first wife he had three sons and two daughters; John, Thomas, Richard, Margaret, who became first the wife of Henry Goodrick, brother of Thomas, Bishop of Ely and Lord Chancellor of England, afterwards of Mr. Crompton, of Stone ; and Catherine, who married Oliver Richardson.

The names of the three sisters of Sir John Rawson were Anne, who became the wife of Richard Cely of London ; Elizabeth, wife of John Foxe, a merchant of London ; and Alice, of whom we have no marriage record.

Having thus far given some account of Sir John and his descendants, together with those of his brothers and sisters, let us look at a brief record of his father, Richard Rawson, who was also a merchant of London, and, in the year 1475, Alderman of Farringdon Extra, and Sheriff of London in 1476. He married Isabella Craford, a descendant of the Crafords of Northumberland. He died in 1483, and was buried at the church of St. Mary Magdalen, Milk street, London. By his will he gave many charitable and devotional legacies, including the church at Fryston and for repairing the highways in and about Pomfret, Sherburn, Fryston and Castleford, in Yorkshire.

Isabella, his wife, died in 1497, and was buried on Milk street by the side of her husband. By her will she gave several legacies, one to the Free Chapel of Gressenhall, County of Norfolk, of which her son Nicholas was master.

Richard, the Sheriff of London, was son of Richard Rawson of Fryston, Yorkshire, England, and grandson of Robert of the same place, who married Agnes the daughter of Thomas Mares, and lived during the time of Richard II., and was probably born previous to the 14th century.

The Rawsons may properly be styled a Yorkshire family. In the Harleian collection of Heralds visitations, at the 'British

Museum, London, England, may be found several pedigrees of different branches of the one great family. All but one appear to be records of the family in Yorkshire, only one being found in the collection of the family in any other County, and that one in Essex, volume 1137, folio 49.

A collection of some of these pedigrees has been made and will be found at the end of this sketch.

Edward Rawson, the grandfather of the Secretary, was a merchant, dealing in silks and woolen goods, and resided in the town of Colnbrook, in the Parish of Langley Marsh, Buckinghamshire, about seventeen miles west of London. Here his children were born. He was a man of considerable property, and died rather early in life. His will was dated February 16, 1603, and proved May 4th the following year. He left two sons, Henry and David, both minors at the time of his death. His wife was Bridget Warde ; she married for a second husband, Thomas Woodward, Esq., of Lincoln's Inn, County of Middlesex.

By the father's will Henry, the eldest son, was to have the house, called the Draggon, and two shops thereunto adjoining all in Colnbrook. This was very likely the store or place of business, where the son might continue in trade as his father's successor. David was to receive 200*l* on his reaching the age of one and twenty, and also at the death of the mother to have the old homestead in Colnbrook. Wife Bridget and son Henry were named as executors. It was also decided that he should learn a trade, and in accordance with the custom of that period, he was bound out for a term of seven years to acquire the art of a tailor. Having served his apprenticeship with Mr. Nathaniel Weston, and reached the appointed age, he received the munificent gift from his father's estate, and established himself in the city of London as a merchant tailor. As the home of his youth was but a very few miles from Windsor, where the Rev. Dr. William Wilson preached, and also situated on the main road between that noted place and the great metropolis, we may imagine that David had met and early made the acquaintance of the Rev. Doctor's daughter Margaret. They may have been brought together at the village school, or at the home of David's father, he being a man of wealth and social standing in the neighborhood. The Wilson family may have been in the habit of calling at the merchant's house, as they must have frequently made trips between Windsor and London. But it matters little at this writing how the first interview was brought about. The facts are that David took the minister Wilson's daughter Margaret to wife and established a home in the great city of London. But that happy home was soon to be despoiled of its charm. Within a few short years the husband and father died, leaving his sorrowing widow, as David's mother had been left, with two small children.

By reading the will of David Rawson,* father of the Secretary, we learn that he was born in Colnbrook, Buckinghamshire, and at the date of the execution of that instrument, was a citizen, and merchant tailor of London ; also that he left three children, two sons and a daughter, namely, William, Edward, and Dorothy. This Edward became the Secretary. David had apparently been successful in business, leaving what might be considered a large estate for his time, and much wisdom and thoughtfulness was displayed in its distribution.

He named as overseers, Thomas Woodward, Esq., his step-father ; his brother, Henry Rawson ; brothers-in-law, Dr. Edmond Wilson, and Rev. John Wilson, the latter afterwards known as minister of the first church in Boston, Mass. The body of the will was drawn June 15, 1616. On the 27th of November, in the year following, a codicil was added, in which the daughter Dorothy was mentioned. Within the next three months the father died, and the will was proved by the widow Margaret, 25 February, 1617.† A few years later the widow married William Taylor of London, a haberdasher or dealer in small wares such as ribbons, tapes, etc. Col. Chester tells us in the Genealogy of the Taylor Family, prepared by him for Mr. P. A. Taylor, that they were married previous to March 23, 1624, for on that day a post-nuptial settlement was dated.

By this marriage she had three children : Edmond Taylor, the eldest, who became a gentleman given to intellectual pursuits, was

* See Appendix.   † At that date the year began in the month of March.

a prominent non-conformist, received in the year 1655 from Oliver Cromwell the appointment of Rector of Littleton, and was for a time imprisoned for the part he took in the Monmouth Rebellion ; he resided in Witham, Essex. A daughter, Margaret Taylor, married 28 January 1640-41, William Webb, a grocer in London. The other child, Hannah, married Robert Clarkson, or Claxton, citizen and merchant draper of London ; marriage articles dated Dec. 22, 1646.

The mother died previous to January 1, 1628, and Mr. William Taylor, her last husband, died 29 June, 1651, at Hackney, where he was buried on the 8th day of July following. He left a very large estate, valued then at 4000*l* (equal to $40,000 now), and gave among other gifts 800*l* to each of his daughters, Mrs. Webb and Mrs. Clarkson. There are no persons by the name of Rawson mentioned in his will.

Margaret, the mother of Secretary Rawson, was daughter of Rev. William Wilson, D. D., of Merton College, Oxford, Prebendary of St. Paul's and Rochester Cathedrals. He held the rectory of Cliffe in the County of Kent, and in the year 1584 became Canon of St. George's Chapel, Windsor Castle ; sister to Edmond Wilson, M. D., of London, who, about the year 1633, gave one thousand pounds sterling to the Colony of Massachusetts Bay ; and the Rev. John Wilson, minister of the first church in Boston ; also grand-niece of Edmond Grindall, D. D., Archbishop of Canterbury.* It would be exceedingly interesting to the descendants of the Secretary, could they have a complete history of his early life while in London with his mother, or at Windsor with his grandparents. The early death of his father, Edward being less than two years of age at the time, may have materially changed the course marked out for the young child. But surrounded as he was by relatives and friends, enjoying the benefits of education, and occupying high positions in life, it is fair to presume that abundant opportunity was given the youth to acquire a reasonable education and lay the foundation for a comparatively useful life.

* Rev. William Wilson, D. D., married Isabel Woodhall, daughter of Elizabeth, a sister of Edmund Grindall, Archbishop of Canterbury.

It does not appear whether or not he had the advantages of a collegiate course, but it is plainly apparent that he was well qualified to occupy with credit, the many prominent positions of trust that in after years fell to his lot. At the time of the publication of the Memorial of the Rawson Family, it was supposed that Gillingham, Dorsetshire, England, was the birthplace of our Secretary, but June 15, 1616, David Rawson, his father, records himself as a citizen and merchant tailor of London.

He evidently had been located there a sufficient length of time to establish his citizenship, and as Edward at that date was but fourteen months old, we may reasonably infer that he was born in London.

The mother was left with ample means for the maintenance of herself and family, and being a woman of culture and refined tastes, she, no doubt, devoted all her energy to the careful training of her little ones.

At the death of the mother the subject of our sketch was about thirteen years of age. Whether the youth remained in the family of Mr. Taylor, or was cared for by the Wilsons, does not appear. Two years later, however, the uncle, Rev. John Wilson, decided to accept the invitation to remove to New England, arriving at Salem, Massachusetts, in the year 1630. Within four years from his departure for New England, the other uncle, Edmond Wilson, M. D., died. One uncle, Henry Rawson, a brother of his father, still remained, residing at the old homestead in Colnbrook, and here young Edward may have passed a few years while attending school.

When John Endicott, the founder of the Colony of Massachusetts, made his adventurous trip with his little company of associates to the shores of New England, Edward Rawson was but a lad of tender years. No doubt he had listened with thorough boyish curiosity to the thrilling stories as they fell from the lips of relatives and friends much older than himself, who felt a special interest in the venture, while they repeated in his presence the numerous reports that came to the people of London and Windsor, of the trials and privations of the little colony in their new home, or expressions of inestimable joy and satisfaction at feeling themselves fairly beyond the restraint of a tyrannical and uncompromising government.

It was natural that such stories should make lasting impressions on the youth's mind, and two years later, when his uncle, Rev. John Wilson, took his departure for the new country, the child must have felt a singularly deep sense of interest in that then, to him, far-away spot, and he may have then wished in his boyish fancy that at some future day his eyes might rest upon that promised land, and his feet press its virgin soil. The deep affection he felt for this uncle, who seemed to him quite like a father, must have also served as a loadstone to attract his attention westward across the Atlantic.

He next appears to us in the town of Gillingham, Dorsetshire, at the home of Mr. Richard Perne, whose daughter Rachel he married. For a brief time the young couple made their home in Gillingham. Their first child was born here. Whether Mr. Perne lived to witness the marriage of his daughter, or not, we cannot say. He died April 11 or 12, 1636, leaving a will executed April 10, in which he named Edward Rawson as one of the overseers, and his wife, Rachel, to be executrix.

Within two years after the death of Mr. Perne, Edward Rawson, with his young wife, left Old England for America, arriving at Newbury, we believe, in the year 1637. April 19, 1638, when but twenty-three years of age, he was chosen Public Notary and Register for that Town, and was annually reëlected until 1647. Many other public trusts and responsible duties were laid upon him by the people of Newbury. As early as the year 1638, he was one of the Deputies to represent the Town at the General Court, and was reëlected for nearly all the successive years to 22 May, 1650, at which time he was chosen Secretary of the Massachusetts Bay Colony, which office he continued to hold for thirty-six years.

Mr. Rawson took his seat as representative from Newbury at the May session, 1638, being the youngest member of that honorable body. In those days the conveniences for traveling to and from

Newbury and Boston were quite different from what they are at the present day. Then the journey was made generally either on foot or horseback, and the traveler was subject to more or less delays by the way, as we may see. On the 8th of June following, he, with several other Deputies were fined five shillings each, for being absent when Court was called. Edward Converse, the ferryman, appeared at the bar and answered for Mr. Rawson's tardiness, and was ordered to pay his fine, and be more careful in the future to have boats manned and in readiness to carry people over the ferry more promptly. Sept. 6, he was appointed by the General Court, Commissioner for the Town of Newbury, and also one of a committee, with Bradstreet and Winthrop, to settle the plantation of Winnicumet, afterwards called Hampton, N. H.; also appointed one of a committee to levy rates or taxes for the Colony.

During subsequent years Mr. Rawson served frequently upon the committee to levy rates, at one time receiving 25 per cent. for collecting customs due the country on wines. June 18, 1645, chosen Clerk of the House of Deputies. Oct. 15, he was one of of a committee to investigate and collect a debt due the country from Mr. Downing and Nehemiah Bourne. 6th of May, 1646, to look after matters at Hampton and at Salisbury, a petition having been presented from some of the inhabitants of the latter place to be a distinct church; and with Samuel Dudley and Edward Carleton, to lay out the bounds of Exeter; to end small causes at Newbury. Nov. 4th of the same year, to examine with the Secretary and see whether or no the Acts of the Court were fairly transcribed to the mind of the Court, and commissioned to see people joined in marriage in Newbury, and given twenty marks expenses for Clerk of the House of Deputies. March, 1647-8, in company with Mr. Hill, to make a review of the Books of Laws, compare amendments, etc. Oct. 27, 1647, he was appointed with Captain Wiggin,* to settle the estate of William Walderne, a bankrupt

* Capt. Thomas Wiggin came to New England invested with authority from Lords Say and Brook, to act as Agent for the settlement at Pascataqua. He made the voyage in the ship James, arriving at Salem Oct. 10, 1633.

debtor, apparently of Dover. May 15, 1649, appointed with Mr. Bellingham, Nowell and Hill, to examine the writings left by Gov. John Winthrop, and put them in proper order; very likely the Journal of Gov. Winthrop that was afterwards published, may have been among the papers referred to. Oct. 14, 1651, appointed Recorder, in place of Mr. Aspenwall, who had been suspended. On petition of Elizabeth, Relict of the late Adam Winthrop, deceased, Mr. Rawson, Thomas Clark and Richard Davenport, were appointed, Oct. 19, 1652, guardians over Adam Winthrop, Jr., to care for his education and estate. Nine days later chosen overseer of the estate of Captain Bozoone Allen, deceased. June 7, 1653, appointed with Richard Bellingham, Thomas Wiggin and Daniel Dennison, to investigate matters to the eastward. The inhabitants at Wells were a little loth to conduct themselves wholly under the rules and regulations laid down by the Colony, and the object of sending this commission of which Mr. Rawson was chosen Secretary, was to soothe the discordant spirits and generate harmony of feeling, and action between the people of Wells and the authorities of the Massachusetts Bay Colony. The mission was fruitful of good results. May 6, 1657, Mr. Rawson was appointed attorney to prosecute in behalf of the Colony, a suit against Richard Woodey. Oct. 19, 1658, chosen one of the Commissioners of Boston. Oct. 21, 1663, an officer to enforce the English Navigation Laws, to look after receiving and delivering proper papers to the ship masters.

The stated salary for Mr. Rawson, as Secretary of the Colony during the first nine years of his service was twenty pounds per annum, a sum that seems rather insignificant from our present standpoint, yet there seems little doubt but that his labors were thoroughly appreciated, and considered at the time reasonably rewarded. The inhabitants of the country were, as a class, poor and unable to pay heavy taxes to support the official representatives of the Colony. In fact, the greater proportion of persons in the colony who held public trusts were those who could, by means of their own estates, give their time and services to the welfare of the Colony, without depending on full remuneration for that service. Many of them not only devoted much time, but also gave considerable sums of money to help forward the well-being of the Colony.

The following, copied from the records of the Massachusetts Bay Colony, will furnish a hint as to what Mr. Rawson did, and how his efforts were appreciated : "Oct. 18, 1659. The court, considering that the Secretary hath served the Country for many years in that place, whose time hath altogether been taken up with the weighty occasions of the country, which have been and are incumbent on him (the neglect whereof would be an inevitable and great prejudice to the public), and himself oft times forced to hire a clerk to help him. which hath cost him some years 20*l* per annum, and every year spending of his own estate a considerable sum beyond what his estate will bear, nor is it for the honor of the country that such an officer, so necessary, who hath also been found faithful and able in the discharge of the trust committed to him, shall want due encouragement, do, therefore, order that the present Secretary shall have from the eleventh day of May last, the sum of 60*l* per annum for his salary, to continue yearly until this Court shall order and provide some other mete recompense."

Nor was this the only measure of requital the Court bestowed upon the honorable Secretary. Many grants of land, amounting in the aggregate to nearly four thousand acres, were from time to time assigned to him for certain special services rendered the Country. Notwithstanding the fact that the duties of the office of Secretary demanded almost his entire time, yet he occasionally was required to give attention to matters that were laid upon him by his associates or towns-people who evidently believed in his ability and trustworthiness to attend to their private business, settling estates, etc. He was one of the overseers of the will of Mr. Henry Webb, a rich Boston merchant, also of the will of Captain Robert Keayne, a wealthy merchant, one of the founders of Massachusetts, and the first commander of that veteran organization in Boston known as the Ancient and Honorable Artillery Company. Captain Keayne's wife was daughter of Sir John Mansfield, and sister to Elizabeth, the wife of Rev. John Wilson, uncle to the Secretary and first minister of Boston, and as the Captain came from London, he evidently had known Edward Rawson from childhood, and it is evidence of his opinion as to the character of his lifelong friend that he was willing to place in his hands the distribution of his valuable estate.

To every person who has had occasion to examine the early records of the Massachusetts Bay Colony, the name of Edward Rawson must be thoroughly familiar. His constancy and faithfulness as clerk is distinctly apparent, while his plain, legible style of penmanship brings at once a sense of relief and satisfaction to all its readers. So thoroughly were his efforts and chirography appreciated that he was early styled an "eloquent inditer."

Mr. Rawson may have possessed peculiarities and individualities, but even by the light of the present day, after making due allowance for his time, the record he has left behind of services rendered will bear comparison with many other of the workers during those early and trying experiences in the life of the Colony.

Dr. Nathaniel B. Shurtleff, of Boston, the antiquary who compiled for publication the early records of the Massachusetts Bay Colony, says in his introduction or preface to that work, "Of all the secretaries of this Colony, none surpassed Mr. Rawson in peculiarities of chirography, and in the use of similar forms for different letters. He had various ways of writing the letters *e* and *r*, very often writing them in such a careless manner that nothing but the context could possibly lead to the discovery of his intentions. In the use of the letters *n*, *u*, *c*, and *t* and *c*, and *l*, he was equally faulty. In a few instances the peculiar style of writing used by Secretary Rawson, such as the condensation of two letters into one, and by an extra stroke of the pen the making of one letter assume the appearance of two has not been followed. Several of the most common instances are the use of an *m* for *nn*, as Pemiman for Penniman, and an *m*, for an *n*, as Haimes for Hines. He seems to have adopted a style of contractions or contracted expressions, or half spelled words."

The Doctor, perhaps, did not intend this so much in the sense of a criticism upon the handwriting of Mr. Rawson, as he did to express or describe his individuality, and the distinctive features of his chirography. For there is scarcely to be found a manuscript two hundred years or more of age that will not exhibit some special characteristic or peculiar trait of the person who wrote it, especially if he were a person capable of originality, or possessed any force of character. Many of these peculiarities or variations in chirography may be accounted for by the fact that the various writers were schooled or educated amid different surroundings and in various parts of Great Britain. Each county in England possesses its own peculiar style of expressions by words, and as the sound of words differ in the several localities, so the arrangement of letters are varied to express those sounds.

Persons who have been engaged in looking up antique genealogical data will, if they have had much experience, recall the various spellings of the same patronymic. It is, perhaps, no wonder that with the vast amount of inditing that Secretary Rawson found to do, he should adopt certain abbreviations or contractions for the purpose of saving time and labor. But his plain, bold style of penmanship has called forth repeated expressions highly complimentary to him.

Having been continued in office by annual elections so many successive terms shows that aside from his fitness for the position he must have been a person of pleasing address, void of guile, reliable both in character and deportment.

Col. Joseph L. Chester, in his Genealogy of the Taylor family, referring to Secretary Rawson, says, " He became one of the most important men in New England. The only blot on his memory was his being among the most forward and relentless of the persecutors of the Quakers, a fact owing perhaps partly to his official position, but which also shows that in spite of his great abilities and his otherwise irreproachable career, he could not escape the popular fanaticism of the time."

By the fact that Mr. Rawson, so soon after arriving at Newbury and taking the Freeman's oath, was among other public trusts, Commissioner for the Trial of Causes, Reviser of the Laws, etc., we may reasonably conclude that he possessed considerable knowledge of the law. This he may have acquired in the office of Thomas Woodward, Esq., of Lincoln's Inn, second husband of his grandmother.

On the news reaching Boston of the death of Charles II., and orders having been received to proclaim James II. King, preparations were made to perform the ceremony with the usual pomp and display customary on such occasions, and on Monday, April 20, 1685, surrounded by the Governor and assistants, all on horseback, with thousands of people and eight foot companies, amid the beating of drums, sounding of trumpets, and the discharge of musketry and cannon, the Proclamation was announced by Mr. Edward Rawson.

The Secretary was certainly a prominent character in the early history of New England, and the value of his services can hardly be over-estimated. Almost from the moment he set foot on American soil, he devoted his time and energy to the furtherance of the best interests of the Town and Colony in which he sought to found a home, and that service was only concluded through the radical change in the government caused by the usurpation of Sir Edmund Andros.

Few if any of the early colonists came of better parent stock than the subject of this sketch. Few of them were better fitted by mental, moral and social training than he to take hold of and carry forward the difficult task of shaping and conducting the course of an infant colony. Of a goodly family, affable, genial, courteous in manner and speech, upright and honorable in all his private dealings, watchful of and faithful in the discharge of every public trust, never swerving from what he considered his direct line of duty, ofttimes through his generosity contributing from his personal estate for the advancement of public service, and reared amid the advantages of wealth, culture and refinement, Edward Rawson was well qualified by nature and education to become a valuable colleague if not a leader in the young colony. That he possessed considerable knowledge of the law in addition to a strongly defined character, is assured to us by the fact that so many matters of great significance were entrusted to him, the successful discharge of which duty required just such qualifications. He bore the honorable title of "gentleman," and no spot on the record seems to indicate that the honor was misplaced.

He is believed to have been connected with the authorship of two books, one a folio, published in the year 1660, entitled "The General Laws and Liberties Concerning the Inhabitants of the Massachusetts," etc., the other, "The Revolution in New England Justified," published in 1691. A portion of the old farm in Newbury where the Secretary first resided has for more than two hundred years borne the appellation of "Rawson's Meadow." The old house, with but few changes, including the ravages of time, was a few years since still standing a silent witness to the joys and sorrows, struggles, discomforts and privations attending the first dozen years of the family in America.

Mr. Rawson sold this house with forty acres of upland and ten acres of meadow, to William Pilsbury, of Dorchester, Dec. 13, 1651, for 100*l.* Soon after removing to Boston, Mr. Rawson purchased of Mr. Theodore Atkinson, January 30, 1653, two and one-half acres of land, on which stood a cottage or tenement, with numerous out-buildings and a garden, including a generous supply of fruit trees. The place had formerly been the property of Mr. William Aspenwall, and evidently bore the air of a pretentious family residence.

This lot was situated between the "street going to Roxbury" on the east, and the Common on the west. A few years after making this purchase, Mr. Rawson opened a street through this land which was regularly named and known as "Rawson's Lane" from 1670 until about 1748, when the name was changed to Bromfield's Lane, afterwards Bromfield Street.

Fifty-five years had intervened since the death of the Secretary and with the change of population and lapse of time, the old associations had somewhat lost their charm. The old was to be put aside for the new, this time the object being to record an expression of esteem for Justice Edward Bromfield, whose residence was situated on "Rawson's Lane." The "street going to Roxbury" was afterwards named "Malborough street," and still later changed to Washington street, and Tremont street now divides the tract of land, once the home of Secretary Rawson, from the Common. There were several out-buildings upon this estate, but the mansion, or dwelling house was situated on the north side of "Rawson's Lane," standing back some distance from, and fronting on the "Broad street going to Roxbury." Surrounding the family mansion was a choice garden, well supplied with fruit-bearing trees, the whole enclosed by a fence. This mansion, with certain out-buildings, including about one acre of land, Mr. Rawson sold, Oct. 25, 1670, to Capt. John Pinchon, of Springfield,* for 1050l., New England money. A number of small lots were also disposed of to various purchasers, aggregating in value 1158l, New England money.

May 6, 1674, Edward and Rachel Rawson deeded a lot 56 x 60, feet, square to their "now eldest son, William." May 23, 1676, they presented him with another lot, 32 x 83 feet, square. It was very likely upon one of these lots that the dry goods store of William Rawson was located, and where for several years he conducted that business.

The Secretary must have built another residence upon some of the land remaining in his possession ; for, from a note found in Mr. Samuel Sewall's diary, it appears that Mr. Rawson had carefully preserved the "Massachusetts books and papers at his house," and on Saturday, March 5, 1686-7, his house was visited by Justices Lynde and Bullivant, and the books and papers above referred to taken by them to the Town House.

Mr. Rawson was fully in sympathy with the inhabitants of Massachusetts, in their decided opposition to the management of that unwelcome and contemptible trio, Andros, Dudley and Randolph. His thorough knowledge of public affairs gave him an opportunity to anticipate the serious harm that might come to the people of New England were they to be curtailed in or deprived of their Charter privileges. He took a firm stand in the interest of the people, and for their convenience, held in his

* Only son of William Pinchon (or Pynchon), Esq., of Springfield. Was Representative, afterwards Major, Assistant and Councillor.

personal custody the books and papers, it may be with the avowed purpose of preventing, so far as he reasonably could, their going into the hands of either Dudley, Andros or Randolph. This yielding up of the State Documents to the justices, was, we believe, the closing act in his long and valuable career as a public servant.

Edward Rawson's wife, Rachel, died before October 11, 1677. He died August 27, 1693. The names of their children and births are as follows :—

NAME.	BORN.	BAPTISED.	DIED.
RACHEL,	1636.		
EDWARD,	1638.		
MARY PERNE,	May 14, 1640.		
DAVID,	May 6, 1644.		
GRINDAL,	Jan'y 23, 1649.		young.
WILLIAM,	May 21, 1651.	May 25, 1651.	
HANNAH,	Oct., 1653.	Oct. 16, 1653.	May 27, 1656.
REBECCA,	Oct. 19, 1654.	Oct. 29, 1654.	
REBECCA,	May 21, 1656.	May 26, 1656.	
ELIZABETH,	Nov. 12, 1657.	Nov. 25, 1657.	
GRINDAL,	Jan'y 23, 1659.	Jan'y 30, 1659.	
JOHN,	1661.	July 14, 1661.	

About twenty years after the marriage in England of Secretary Rawson, Widow Rachel Perne died, leaving a will bearing date March 31, 1656, and proved the 13th of November following. By this instrument we learn that at the time of her death she was in possession of a living in the Parish of Gillingham, Dorsetshire, called Easthaimes, by lease granted under the hand and seal of William Lord Stowerton, or Stourton, during the reign of King Charles I.* This lease, which included several other valuable pieces of land located in the same vicinity, was to hold for ninety-nine years from date. She made her son, John Perne, executor, and gave her daughter, Rachel Rawson, in New England, forty pounds. Mrs. Rawson's grandfather, John Hooker, was uncle to Rev. Thomas Hooker, that celebrated Divine who

* Will dated Oct. 12, 12th year of the reign of Charles I.

was pastor of the church in Newtown, Mass., and Hartford, Conn. Widow Perne's maiden name appears to have been Green.

To show the manliness of the Secretary and his disposition to carry out so far as possible, certain promises made by him, we would refer to a deed given in trust to Thomas Danforth et al. The document is recorded in Lib. III., pages 413, 414 and 415 of Suffolk Deeds. By this instrument we learn that Edward Rawson was to receive with the hand of Rachel Perne, three hundred pounds, as a marriage portion, from Richard Perne, her father, and that Mr. Rawson was to add six hundred pounds from his own funds to that sum, and with the nine hundred pounds purchase lands, which estate was by jointure to have been settled on his wife, so that in the event of his early demise (as had been the case with Edward's father and grandfather, a precaution well taken) the widow, Rachel, might be properly cared for. Mr. Perne, however, died before completing his part of the agreement, and Mr. Rawson very soon resolved to remove with his wife and children to New England, at which time he gave his word to his mother Perne, that, upon payment by her of the remaining portion of the three hundred pounds, he would make over, in houses and lands in New England for the benefit of his wife and her heirs by him, the value of the said three hundred pounds.

Now on the 21st day of December, 1660, having some eighteen years previous received the money from Mrs. Perne, he executes a mortgage deed of his homestead to Thomas Danforth, Edmond Batter and Samuel Torrey, as friends, in trust for the use of his wife, Rachel, in case of his decease, the same being valued at three hundred pounds. This was the same property he purchased of Theodore Atkinson about seven years previous, paying therefor one hundred and eighty pounds, showing the increase in the value of real estate during that number of years to have been quite marked, although he had made considerable improvement in the way of buildings, etc., the amount of which we cannot judge.

It was provided, however, in this agreement that during Mr. Rawson's life he might sell or dispose of this property, provided always that he placed other sufficient security in its stead in the hands of said trustees. It was also provided that at any time during the life of Mr. Rawson, he might, or at his death his executors or administrators might release this property by paying two hundred and fifty pounds in good current pay equivalent to money, into the hands of said trustees, together with a certain list of articles, valued at fifty pounds. As the articles named give some idea of the style in which the family lived at that time, we will insert the list here.

The two best feather beds; two best boulsters; two best pillows and pillow beers of the finest Holland; four pair best sheets; two of the best rugs, and two blankets; the best red serge curtains and valiants; ye needle work cushon and table cloth; six leather chairs; ye best lookingglass and my great bible; my silver tankard; silver bowl and wine bowl and seven silver spoons; my watch; my cupboard and case of drawers; my great kettle of brass; brass pot and iron pot; one pair tongs and fire pan; one spitt; one skillett; the best trunk; my best beaver hat.

On the 10th day of May, 1664, by mutual consent, another deed was executed to the trustees to take the place of the one previously given.

Notwithstanding the fact that Secretary Rawson at one time was the owner of a large property, consisting of some six thousand acres of land, on a portion of which were valuable improvements, situated in and out of Boston, yet, when the time came to settle his estate, so much of the property had previously been distributed among the heirs, or dispensed in some form or other, that the portion remaining in his name was not sufficient to pay his debts in full. At the time of his death he was doubtless making his home with his son William, at Dorchester.

*Letters of Administration granted unto William Rawson, on the estate of his father, Edward Rawson, late of Boston. Gent. Deceased.

William Stoughton, Esq., commissionated by his Excy, Sir William Phips, K^{nt} Captain General and Governour in Chief in and

* Suffolk Probate Records, Vol. XIII, 323.

over their Maj^tie^ Province of the Massachusetts Bay, in New England, with the advise and consent of the council for the granting of Probate of Wills and Letters of Administration within the County of Suffolk, etc. To William Rawson, son of Edward Rawson, late of Boston, within the said County, Gent Deceased. Intestate, Greeting. Trusting in your care and fidelity, I do, by these presents, commit unto you full power to administer all and singular, the goods, chattels, rights and credits of the said deceased, and well and faithfully to dispose of the same according to law, and also to ask, gather, levy, recover and receive all and whatsoever credits of the said Deceased, which to him while he lived, and at the time of his death did appertain. And to pay all debts in which the deceased stood bound, so far as his goods chattels, rights and credits of the said Deceased. And to exhibit the same unto the Registers office of the aforesaid County of Suffolk, at or before the forth day of April next ensuing, and to render a plain and true account of your said administration upon oath, at or before the forth day of January 1694–5. And I do, by these presents, ordain, constitute and appoint you administrator of all and singular the goods, chatels, rights and credits aforesaid.

In testimony whereof I have hereunto set my hand and the seal of the said office. Dated at Boston, the forth day of January, 1693–4.

WILLIAM STOUGHTON.

Isa. Addington, Reg., Esq.

———

Dorchester, 2d Feby, 1693–4.

An inventory taken of the goods and estate of Mr. Ed Rawson, late deceased, which are now in the hands of William Rawson, administrator, is as followeth, viz :—

Imps. 740 acres of wast land lying betwixt Medfield and Mendon,	37	0	0*
It one bed and bedding, with appertences,	4	6	0
" wearing apparel both woolen and linen,	5	6	6

* Valued at about twenty-five cents an acre.

"   an old skreen with other small lumber,   0   3   6
"   Plate, buttons and buckles,   10   6
"   three old books, two sachells, a p^r spectacles,   8   8
pr. John Wilson, James Bracket,   47   15   2
what is in my bro, Grindall's hands as by a/c of the
    particulars, by him valued   3   8   0

               Total,   51   3   2

WILLIAM RAWSON.

Appeared and made oath to its accuracy before William Stoughton, Boston, February 21, 1694–5.*

William Rawson represented that he finds the estate insolvent, and Sampson Sheafe, merchant, Benjamin Walker and Thomas Banister, shop keepers, all of Boston, were appointed by William Stoughton, on April 6, 1695, commissioners to receive and examine all claims against the estate and report list of the same to Mr. Stoughton, at Register office, that due proportion may be distributed on the claims as the estate will pay.†

* Suffolk Probate Records, Vol. XIII., 556.
† Suffolk Probate Records, Vol. XIII., 578.

WILL OF EDWARD RAWSON,

Grandfather of the Secretary.

EDWARD RAWSON, of Colbrooke, in the Parish of Langley Marris in the County of Buckingham, mercer, 16 February, 1603, proved 4 May, 1604.

To my wife, Bridget Rawson, for and during her natural life, my house and tenement and the appurtenances, &c., lying in Colbrooke, now in the occupation of Edward Whitlock, and after her decease, unto David Rawson, my son, and to the heirs male of his body lawfully begotten : and for want of such issue unto Henrie Rawson, my eldest son, and to the heirs male of his body lawfully begotten : and failing such issue, to the right heirs of me the said Edward, forever.

To son Henry all that house called the "Draggon" and the two shops thereunto adjoining, lying and being in Colbrooke aforesaid, and to his heirs male &c., with remainder to son David and his lawful issue, &c., and failing such issue unto Ralphe Ward, my brother-in-law, and his heirs forever.

To the said David Rawson, my son, the sum of two hundred pounds at his full age of one and twenty years. Henry Rawson, also a minor. My executors at their cost and charge shall bring up my son David in some reasonable learning until he may be fitt to be putt to apprentice unto some good trade or mystery. My brother Henry Rawson doth owe me fifty pounds. Wife Bridgett and son Henry to be executors, and John Bowser, gentleman, Ralph Ward, Philip Bowreman and George Charley to be overseers.

—*Vol. 39, page 308, N. E. Hist. and Gen. Register.*

WILL OF DAVID RAWSON,

Father of the Secretary.

DAVID RAWSON, Citizen and merchant tailor of London, a most unworthy servant of Jesus Christ, 15 June, 1616, proved by his widow Margaret Rawson, 25 February, 1617. . My goods, &c., shall be divided into three equal and just parts and portions according to the laudable custom of this honorable city of London. One of the three parts to Margaret Rawson, my loving and well beloved wife. One other part to William and Edward Rawson, and such other child or children as I shall hereafter have or as my wife shall be with child withall at the time of my decease, to be equally divided amongst them all, part and part alike. The third part I reserve towards the payment of legacies, gifts, and bequests, &c, To William Rawson, my eldest son, a double gilt salt and a standing cup with a cover, double gilt, and half a dozen of Postle spoons and two double gilt spoons, and a silver porringer, a silver spoon and a silver bowl. To Edward Rawson, my son, a great standing bowl, double gilt, and six spoons, and two double gilt spoons, "which was given him by those which were his witnesses at his christening," and a silver bowl. All the rest of the plate to my wife. To the relief of the poor of the town of Colbrooke, in the County of Buckingham, where I was born, the sum of five pounds of lawful money of England, to be paid within one year next after my decease. To John Emery, son of John Emerie of Colbrooke, clark, deceased, five pounds, to be paid him on the day when he shall be made a freeman of the City of London. To William Fenner, a poor scholar in Pembroke Hall in Cambridge, five pounds within three years after my decease. To David Anngell, my godson, five pounds at the age of twenty one years. To John Nayle, the son of Nicholas Nayle, of Iver, in the County of Buckingham, five pounds on the day he shall be made a freeman of the City of London, if he take good courses. To the poor people at my funeral the sum of forty shillings. To

John Anngell, clothworker, forty pounds, and to Alexander
Dubber, clothworker, forty shillings, which I will shall be de-
ducted out of such money as he shall owe me at the time of
my decease (if any be). Item, I give unto my godson, Edward
Rawson, the son of my brother, Henry Rawson, the sum of ten
pounds to be paid him at his age of twenty one years.

I give and bequeath to my dear mother, Bridgett Woodward,
the sum of ten pounds, which I desire her to give to Mr. Winge
and Mr. Foxe, forty shillings a piece, if she so please. To my
sister-in-law, Jane Rawson, the sum of forty shillings to make her
a ring, and to my sister-in-law, Isabel Gibbs, the like sum of forty
shillings to make her a ring, and to my sister-in-law, Elizabeth
Wilson, the like sum of forty shillings to make her a ring; which
said four legacies so given to my mother and three sisters I will
shall be paid within one year next after my decease. Item, I do
give and bequeath to my brother-in-law, Thomas Wilson, the sum
of five pounds, to be paid within one year, &c., and to Andrew
Warde, son of my uncle, Ralphe Warde, the sum of five pounds,
to be paid him at his age of twenty one; and to my uncle, John
Warde, the sum of forty shillings, if he be living at my decease.
To my master, Mr. Nathaniel Weston, the sum of forty shillings
to make a ring, and I desire him to be assisting to my executrix
to help get in my debts. To Isabel Sheafe, three pounds to be
bestowed in a piece of plate and given her·at her age of twenty
one years or at the day of her marriage, which ever shall first
happen. To my son, Edward Rawson, over and above his said
part, the sum of one hundred pounds; and to my apprentice,
Matthew Hunte, the sum of six pounds thirteen shillings and four
pence, to be paid to him on the day he shall be made a freeman
of the City of London; and to William Beard and John Sanford,
my apprentices, (the like sums on the like conditions). If all
my children die the portions shall remain & come to Alexander
Rawson, the eldest son of my said brother Henry Rawson, (if he
be then living): but if he die then to John Rawson and Edward
Rawson, two other of the children of my said brother, &c., equally.
The Residue to wife Margaret and son William. I constitute my
loving friends, Mr. Thomas Woodward of Lincoln's Inn, in the

County of Middlesex, Esq., my father-in-law, my brother, Henry Rawson, and Edmond Wilson, Doctor of Physic, and John Wilson, Master of Arts, my brothers-in-law, oversears, and give them five pounds apiece. If wife should die then the above to be executors during the minority of my said sons William and Edward. Witnessed by John Wilkinson and Arthur Viger ser.

In a codicil made 27 November, 1617, he bequeaths to daughter Dorothy Rawson besides her (child's) portion the sum of one hundred pounds at her age of twenty one or day of marriage ; to sister Anne Wilson, the wife of brother Thomas Wilson, the sum of forty shillings ; to Uncle John Warde the sum of seven pounds thirteen shillings and four pence and some of my cast apparell ; to my cousin, Elizabeth Glover, the sum of twenty shillings ; to cousin Jane Lawrence twenty shillings ; to Isabel Cave twenty shillings ; to Aunt Fenner ten shillings ; to Mr. Frogmorton forty shillings ; to Mr. Houlte twenty shillings ; to Mrs. Jane Bartlett ten shillings ; to Mrs. Martin of Windsor ten shillings ; to cousin Dorothy Sheafe a piece of plate of fifty three shillings price ; all these legacies to be paid within one year and a half next after my decease by my executrix. Codicil witnessed by John Wilkinson and John Hill.

RAWSON PEDIGREE.

Robert Rawson of Frystone,=Agnes, dau. Thomas Mares.
Yorkshire, was living in
the time of Richard II.
(1377.)

Richard Rawson of Frystone=Cecily, dau. of Palden or Baldein.
Will dated May 14, 1473, proved
Sept. 9, 1475.

A (See p. 32.)

Richard Rawson,=Isabella	Robert	Henry	Elizabeth,	Katharine	Ellen
citizen & mercer	Craford,	Rawson,	Rawson,	m. 1st, Long-	Rishworth.	Aylmer
of London; al-	d. 1497,	had dau.	resid. leg.	ley; 2d, Shaws.		or Elmer.
derman of Far-	buried at	Cecile.	in his	Had son, Pat-		
ringdon extra, 14	St. Mary		mother's	rick Longley.		
Edward IV.	Magd.,		will, 1475.		
Sheriff of Lon-	Milk st.			
don in 1476.	London.			

B (See p. 33.)

Avery Rawson=

Nicholas Rawson=Beatrix, dau. of Sir Philip Cooke, Knight of Gidea Hall, Essex, and
widow of Wm. Copley, Esq. She d. Jan. 14, 1554. Buried at
Shelford, Notts.

Walter Rawson,	Philippa,	Margaret,	Sir Michael Stanhope=Anne, born 1512;
died without	b. 1507.	b. 1510.	Knight of Shelford,	died Feb. 20, 1587;
issue.			Notts. Steward 1544.	buried at Shelford,
			Gov. of Hull 1547.	Notts.

Chief Gentleman of the Privy
Chamber to the King, 1548.
Beheaded Feb. 26, 1552.

—Sir Thomas Stanhope of Shelford, died 1596.

—Edward Stanhope, Esq., one of the Queen's Council in the North of Eng. d. 1608.

—Sir John Stanhope of Harrington. Gentleman of the Privy Chamber to Queen Elizabeth; created Lord Stanhope of Harrington 1605.

—Edward Stanhope, D. C. L. and Master in Chancery.

—Sir Michael Stanhope of Sudbourne, Gentleman of the Privy Chamber to Queen Elizabeth.

—Eleanor Stanhope.

—Julyan, w. Sir John Hotham.

—Jane.

—William and Edward, Died in infancy.

Rawson Pedigree, (continued).

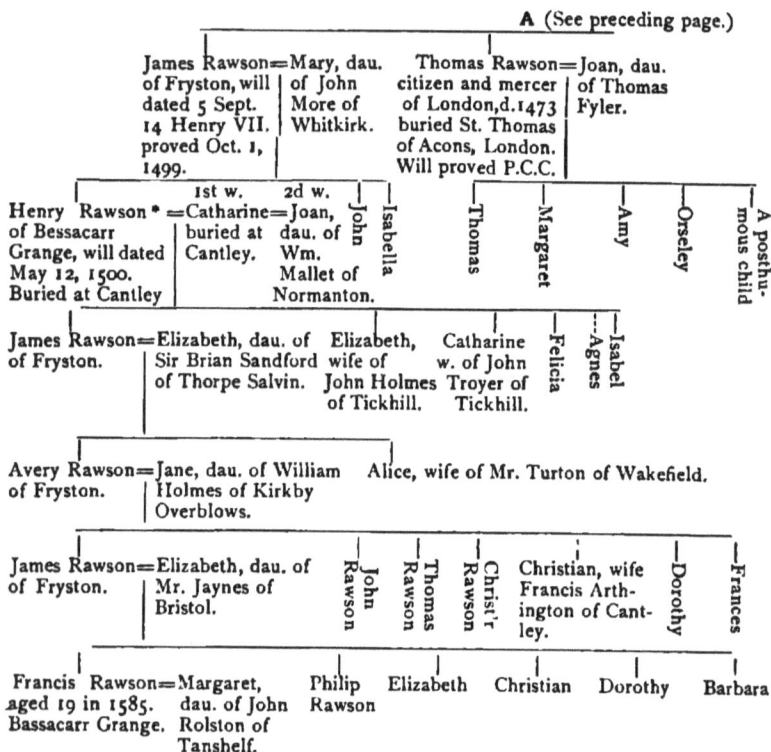

A (See preceding page.)

James Rawson=Mary, dau. | Thomas Rawson=Joan, dau.
of Fryston, will | of John | citizen and mercer | of Thomas
dated 5 Sept. | More of | of London, d. 1473 | Fyler.
14 Henry VII. | Whitkirk. | buried St. Thomas
proved Oct. 1, | | of Acons, London.
1499. | | Will proved P.C.C.

	1st w.	2d w.	John	Isabella	Thomas	Margaret	Amy	Orseley	A posthumous child
Henry Rawson *	=Catharine	=Joan,							
of Bessacarr	buried at	dau. of							
Grange, will dated	Cantley.	Wm.							
May 12, 1500.		Mallet of							
Buried at Cantley		Normanton.							

James Rawson=Elizabeth, dau. of | Elizabeth, | Catharine | Felicia | Agnes | Isabel
of Fryston. | Sir Brian Sandford | wife of | w. of John
of Thorpe Salvin. | John Holmes | Troyer of
| of Tickhill. | Tickhill.

Avery Rawson=Jane, dau. of William | Alice, wife of Mr. Turton of Wakefield.
of Fryston. | Holmes of Kirkby
| Overblows.

James Rawson=Elizabeth, dau. of | John Rawson | Thomas Rawson | Christ'r Rawson | Christian, wife | Dorothy | Frances
of Fryston. | Mr. Jaynes of | | | | Francis Arth-
| Bristol. | | | | ington of Cant-
| | | | | ley.

Francis Rawson=Margaret, | Philip | Elizabeth | Christian | Dorothy | Barbara
aged 19 in 1585. | dau. of John | Rawson
Bassacarr Grange. | Rolston of
| Tanshelf.

* In the reign of Henry VII., Henry Rawson was living at Bessacarr Grange, Cantley, West Riding, a parish lying southerly and a short distance from Doncaster, county of York. In his will, made May 12, 1500, he expressed the wish that his body should be buried in the church of Cantley, near those of his wives Catharine and Joan. His grandson Avery, or Averey, obtained June 2, 1557, a grant of what the monks had once enjoyed here. It is supposed that the Rawsons abandoned Bessacarr about the year 1603, or soon after the beginning of the reign of King James I. Hugh and William Rawson were governors of goods and possessions of the Free Grammar School of King James of England at Suffield; and one Thomas Rawson, perhaps the son of Avery above, was head master of this school for many years, beginning previous to the year 1629, and continuing until his death in 1645; and only absent while fleeing from the Earl of Newcastle's army, May 5, 1643, returning to his charge again as soon as the siege was laid against Sheffield Castle, August 3, 1644.

B (See page 31.)

Christopher = 1st, Margaret.
Rawson, = 2d, Agnes,
citizen and | dau. Wm.
merchant of | Buke
London,
died 1518

Sir John
Rawson,
Knight
of Rhodes
and of St.
John of
Jerusalem;
Lord Treas.
of Ireland,
d. 1560.

Richard
Rawson,
D.D.,LL.B.
Canon of
Windsor,
d. 1543.

Nicholas
Rawson,
·Master
of the
Free
Chapel
of Gres-
senhall,
Norfolk.

Anne
Salle
or Selye,
wife of
Richard
Cely.

Elizabeth
wife of
John
Foxe,
merchant
of London.

Alice

Catharine, wife of
Rowland Whyte.

John   Walter

Margeret,
wife of John
Kettleby.

Isabella,
wife of
1st, Robert
Warham,
gent.; 2d,
Anthony
Cooke, Esq.
of Averly,
Essex.

John
Rawson.

Thomas
Rawson.

Richard
Rawson.

Margaret
wife of 1st,
Henry
Goodrick;
2d, Mr.
Crompton.

Catharine
wife of
Oliver
Richardson.

Henry =

Edward = Bridget Warde.
merchant | She m. 2d, Thos. Wood-
at Coln- | ward, Esq. of Lincoln's
brook, Co. | Inn, Co. Middlesex.
Buck.
d. 1604.

Isabel = — Gibbs.

Henry = Jane —
Colnbrook |
Co. Bucks. |

David = Margaret, dau.
Merchant | Rev. Wm. Wil-
Tailor in | son; sister to
London, | Rev. John Wil-
d. 1618. | son, minister
1st Ch, Boston.

Alexander   John   Edward

William

Edward = Rachel, dau.
b. 1616.   Richard & Rachel
Secretary Mass. Bay Colony.   (Greene†) Perne.

Dorothy

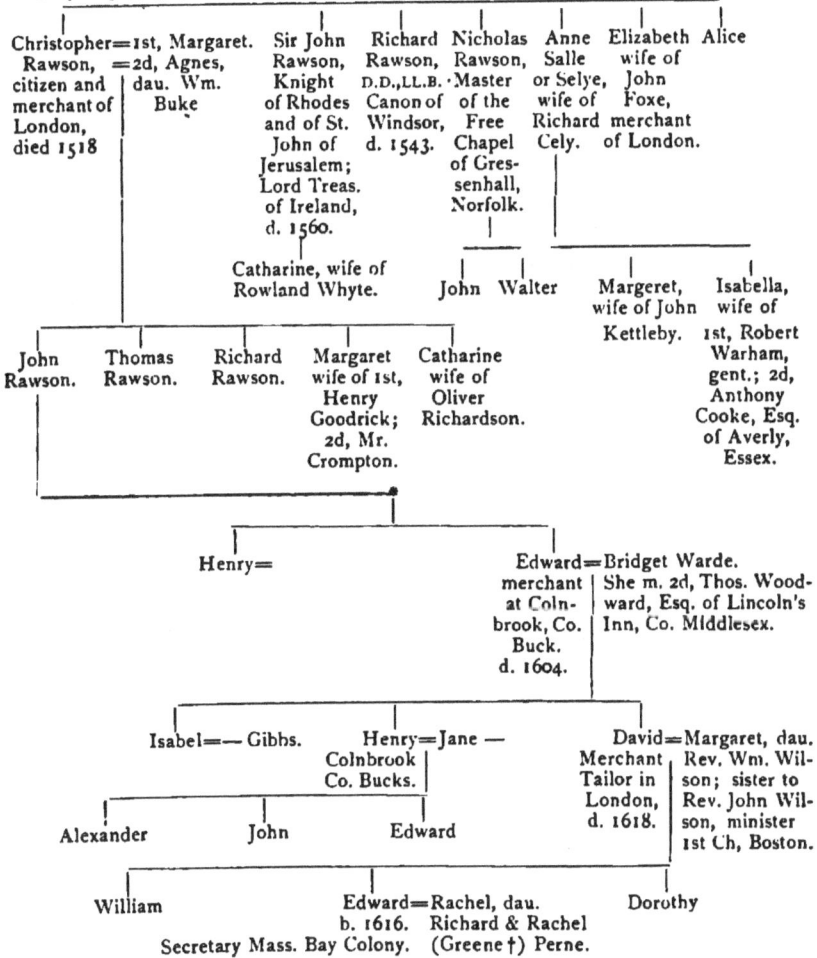

* During the past two years the writer has been living in suspense, yet constantly encouraged by the hope that possibly the *next* mail from England would bring to hand the information sought. But we regret to note here, that a careful search among the records in and about London, has failed thus far to reveal the missing link that connects the grandfather of our Secretary with the foregoing pedigree. Yet there seems no good reason for doubting the family connection. To present an unbroken chain of family descent for five hundred years, consisting of eighteen or nineteen generations, has been the object of my research.

† She was a daughter of Richard and Mary (Hooker) Greene, and sister of John Greene, Surgeon of Warwick, R. I., who died in 1658 or 1659.

ADDENDA.

The Rawsons may properly be styled a Yorkshire family. Nearly all the pedigrees that have been collected by the heralds and deposited among the collections of visitations at the British Museum, London, England, that bear the name of Rawson were collected from the county of York, and mainly from that portion of the county known as West Riding. As far back in the past as this patronymic can be traced, we find its birthplace at Fryston. The present spelling of the name has been traced backward more than five hundred years, or to about A. D. 1350, at which time Robert Rawson, who heads our family pedigree, was born. An old tradition exists in England that the family are descended from the Saxon family of Ravenchil, who, long before the Norman conquest, were located in the valley of the river Aire. The Domesday Book certainly mentions the name of Ravenchil as a person in possession of land and other property in Yorkshire about the year 1086. From this source the name would come through Rauenchil, Ravenchil, Ravenson, Rawson. But this tradition may have been suggested by the raven's head used by some as a crest to the family armorial. Mark Antony Lower, M. A., F. S. A., who is most excellent authority on the origin of English surnames, tells us that the name comes from Raulf, Raulfo, Ralph, through Rawes and Rawson, the latter meaning son of Rauf or Rawes.

There are four pedigrees on record in the British Museum, relating to the Rawsons of Besacle or Cantley, county of York, reference to which is as follows : 1394, p. 264 ; 1415 fo., 33 b. ; 1420 fo., 189 b. ; 1487 fo., 81 b.

Two of the family of Pigborne, or Pickburn, 1420 fo. 218 b., 4630, p. 478. One at Shipley, 4630, p. 482. One of the family in Essex county, 1137, fo. 49. But the latter seems to be an offshoot from the Yorkshire family. One or two centuries ago the family were quite prominent and numerous about the parish of Sheffield, Brookside and Wardsed in West Riding, Pickburn in the parish of Brodsworth, Bessacarr Grange, Nidd Hall and Bradford, Hope House and Mill House, all of these places being located in the southern portion of the county of York, England. While as a family the Rawsons may not have produced very many strikingly prominent, or what might be termed brilliant or distinguished men, yet a generous proportion of persons bearing that name have been found among the expounders of religion, and apparently have done what they could to reclaim and elevate the standard of society wherever their lot may have been cast.

As it may prove interesting to some of the family to know of the dreadful experience that some of their kin were forced to pass through during a period of Cromwell's famous career, we will repeat the story of Thomas Rawson, M. A., who was admitted rector of All Saints parish, at Hoby in the county of Leicester, July 6, 1642. His wife was Lydia, daughter of Sir Roger Nevison, Knight, a lady of high birth and education. The parish proved an interesting and enjoyable one, and the associations for both pastor and people were extremely pleasant until the breaking out of the Rebellion, when he was forced to retire and secrete himself to avoid persecution through the miseries of a prison cell. Mr. Rawson was soon despoiled of his living here, and it was given to one Smith, who, on being denied possession of the parsonage, Mrs. Rawson and her children still residing there, procured from Leicester a party of horse, and returning, inhumanly dragged her from the house and left her in the church yard. For several days and nights Mrs. Rawson and her children remained in the church porch and belfry, until Mr. Needham, rector of Rotherby, on learning of the affair, allowed them to reside in his parsonage, where for a time they were made comfortable. But soon Mr. Needham's turn came, and he was ejected from his parish. She was now compelled to find refuge in the church porch at Rotherby. After a time however, she was allowed to occupy the belfry, blankets being hung up to serve as a screen between the family and the congregation. Here they remained some time until Sir Thomas Hartopp gave them the privilege of dwelling in some outhouses belonging to a tenement he owned in Rotherby. These outhouses were cheap structures, there being no stairs connecting the lower with the upper rooms, ladders being used as a substitute. Here, in these miserable quarters, Mrs. Rawson and her nine or ten children subsisted on the charity of friends and neighbors. At length the family were returned to Hoby and cared for, the record says, *by law*, although they were crowded into a wretched house with but one room in it. The parish soon bound out one of the children to a lace-maker; two others were cared for at the house of a neighbor. Sir Henry Hudson, of Milton Mowbry, took two of them, and two more were soon taken by Matthias Wolfe, the lacemaker, who had the other brother. One of the boys, George by name, being lame, was placed by the parish in a hospital where he could receive proper treatment.

The fortunes of war always bring direful effects, but the fortunes of a civil war are ofttimes dreadful in the extreme. The privations and hardships undergone by this family were severe indeed. Mrs. Rawson was a lady of rank, born in high life, and accustomed to enjoy all the advantages of wealth and social position, and consequently unprepared to cope with such hardships. The husband on whom she leaned for sympathy and support was obliged to remain in seclusion until such time as the reaction of public sentiment should come. While Mrs. Rawson and her children were living in that wretched room, they were seen by the neighbors standing around a sieve of horse beans, eating them out of their hands, having not even a pewter dish, or a spoon of any kind, or so much as a wooden bowl. They were without a table, chair or stool. During this wretched experience two children were born, but the mother died at the birth of the last one.

No one about Hoby knew where Mr. Rawson went or what he did during this long suspense. He must however, have made visits to his family now and then. After the Restoration he was repossessed of his benefice, but the strain had been too great, and within a year he died beloved by all who knew him.

According to the journal of the House of Commons, Lydia, wife of Mr. Thomas Rawson, minister of Hoby, obtained one-fifth part of the profits of the parsonage in the year 1645.

Whether Mr. Rawson was in sympathy with the King or with Parliament does not appear in the record, leaving us to query whether he fled before the cavaliers of King Charles when they took possession of West Riding and plundered the larger towns, or whether he retired before the presence of the Parliamentary forces under the Earl of Essex, when they marched forth to the protection of the Puritans in that locality.

The parish of Brodsworth is situated in West Riding, county of York, and was the abode of a distinguished family who took their name from it. Subsequently it descended to a family by the name of Awaston, and about the year 1600 Pickburn, a township in this parish, came into the possession of John Rawson, who made the estate his abode until his death, which occurred in 1623 at the age of 47 years. The estate remained in the family for nearly one hundred years. The Rawsons were generous patrons of St. Michael's Church at Brodsworth, and a window there bears the family coat of arms.

The following is the pedigree by William Dugdale :

John Rawson=Alice, dau. Barmly Vicars,
d. 1623, a. 47 | Oct. 14, 1600, buried 23 Aug., 1630.
  |

John=Ursula, dau. John Rawson of Carcroft, Co. York.
d. Mch. | m. Feb. 1617-18.
28, 1628 |
  |

John=Mary, dau. Darcy Wash- Catharine   Ann   William
aged 40 | ington of Adwick-lo-Street,
Sept. 14 | Esq. m. 17 April, 1651.
1665. | Buried June 4, 1694.
d. 25 |
Mch. |
1679. |
  |

Richard, Darcy*=Sarah — Thomas Anne Ursula William
a. 12 1665,
d. 2 July, 1696. |
  |

Darcy, bapt.   Ursula, bapt.   Elizabeth, bapt.
25 Feb. 1697-8.   May 9, 1696.   12 Dec. 1699.
Living in 1708.

* Darcy was 4 years old in 1665. Will dated 5 April, 1708.

STANHOPES CONNECTED WITH THE RAWSONS.

The family of Stanhope took their name from a town of that name situated in the bishopric of Durham, where the family resided previous to their removing to Nottinghamshire. Sir Richard de Stanhope owned a large estate at the North during the middle and early portion of the thirteenth century. His son, Sir Richard, was Lord of Estwyke in Northumberland, and Mayor of Newcastle; and in consideration of his services against the Scots, was granted by King Edward III. one third part of the village and fishery of Paxton, in Scotland. His son, Sir John, fixed his residence in Nottinghamshire, and became the owner of a number of large estates. Edward, the successor of John, was one of the king's principal commanders at the battle of Stoke, near Newark upon Trent, in the year 1487; and also when the Cornish rebels were defeated at Blackheath in 1497. That same year he was made a knight, also Steward of Wakefield, Constable of Sandale Castle in the County of York, and Sheriff of Nottinghamshire and Derbyshire. He died in the year 1512. On the death of Richard, who died without issue, his brother Michael became chief of the family, and obtained from King Henry VIII., in the year 1538, a grant of Eveshall Forest, and of the house and site of the monastery of Shelford, in the same county, the almshouses, &c., within it, and other lands thereunto belonging; also the manor of Shelford with its members, parcel of the possessions of the dissolved monastery there, with several rectories in the counties of Nottingham, Lincoln and Derby. In 1544, he was constituted the king's steward of the great lordship of Holderness and Cottingham in the county of York. Two years later he was knighted by the king, and appointed Governor of Hull. In 1547 he became chief gentleman of the privy chamber, and one of the knights of the shire for the county of Nottingham. But in 1551, without any reason alleged, he was committed prisoner to the Tower with the Duke of Somerset, the Duke's wife, Anne, being his half-sister, and the relationship being thought sufficient ground for concluding him guilty. Accordingly, when the Duke was released, Sir Michael was also given his liberty without accusation. Two years afterwards however, he was again imprisoned with the Duke and Duchess, tried, and it is said on the evidence of one Crane, was found guilty of conspiring the death of a privy councillor, and sentenced to die; and was beheaded on Tower Hill, about a month after the Duke of Somerset had suffered the same penalty, Sir Michael protesting his innocence to the last, in the most solemn manner. William Playfair, Esq., in his elaborate work entitled British Family Antiquity,* shows with a considerable degree of success that Somerset was blameless of the charges made against him, and says if the Duke was blameless "it is still more evident that Stanhope was so."

Sir Thomas, eldest son of Sir Michael, was Sheriff of Nottinghamshire in 1574, and of both Nottinghamshire and Derbyshire in 1582, and knight of the shire for the former of these counties. He died in 1596. His eldest son, Sir John, resided in Elvaston where he died in 1610, having been knighted at Belvoir Castle in 1603 by King James. Sir Philip, his son and heir, was knighted at Whitehall, Dec. 16, 1605, created Baron Stanhope of Shelford in 1616, and in 1628 advanced to the dignity of Earl of Chesterfield. On the breaking out of the civil war between King Charles I. and the Parliament, after using all his influence in vain to reconcile the two parties, he at last, with his sons, joined the royal cause, and having been taken prisoner in March, 1643, continued in confinement until his death in 1656. By a second marriage he had a son who was ancestor to the Earls Stanhope. By his first marriage, to Catharine, daughter of Francis Lord Hastings, he had eleven sons and two daughters. Henry Lord Stanhope, K. B., married Catharine, daughter of Thomas Lord Walton, and died in 1634, leaving two daughters and a son Philip. Lady Stanhope was created by King Charles II. Countess of Chesterfield for life. Philip, Earl of Chesterfield, born in 1634, was appointed in 1662, Lord Chamberlain to Queen Catharine, Colonel of a regiment of foot in 1667, and Lord Warden and Lord Chief Justice of all the King's forests and parks, &c., on

---

* That work is the authority for this sketch of the Stanhope family.

this side Trent in 1669, and appointed Colonel of the third regiment of foot in 1680, which office he resigned in 1685. He died at the age of 81 years, in Bloomsbury Square in 1713, leaving a son Philip, third Earl of Chesterfield, who was born in 1673, and died January, 1726. His successor was Philip, the fourth Earl, born 1695, and educated at Trinity Hall Cambridge. He died in 1773, having distinguished himself by his eloquence on many occasions in Parliament, and was noted for his wit and rare abilities. He was succeeded by Charles Stanhope, who was born in 1755, and was a descendant from Arthur, sixth son of Sir Philip, the first earl.

Arthur, the youngest son of Philip, the first Earl, by wife Catharine Hastings, who settled at Stoke and at Mansfield, was member of Parliament from Hottingham at the time of the restoration of King Charles II., and also in the Long Parliament. He married Anne, daughter of Sir Henry Sailsbury of Lewenny, County of Denbigh, by whom he had three sons, Philip and Henry, who died in infancy, and Charles, who married Frances Topp, by whom he had five sons and four daughters : 1. Francis, died unmarried ; 2. Michael, D. D., Canon of Windsor ; 3. Henry ; 4. Charles ; 5. Topp. Gertrude and Mary died unmarried ; Catharine and Elizabeth both married. Charles, the fourth son, married Cecilia, daughter of Dutton Stede, of Stedehill, in Kent, and had Edwin Francis Stanhope, Esq., Gentleman-usher of the Privy Chamber, and Equerry to the Queen. He died May 16, 1807, leaving two children by wife Catharine, eldest daughter of John, Marquis of Caernarvon : 1. Catharine, who married Sir Hungerford Hoskyns, of Harewood in Herefordshire ; 2. Hon. Edwyn Stanhope, who after obtaining a very thorough education at Easthill, Wandsworth, and Winchester College, entered the service of the navy in 1768, on board the Rose, of 20 guns, under the command of Capt. Caldwell, and sailed for America. Soon after reaching Boston he was transferred to the Romney, under Commodore Hood. In 1771 he was a midshipman on board the Chatham under Vice-Admiral Parry, commander-in-chief at the Leeward Islands. Ill health now compelled him to return to

Europe, but in 1775 he rejoined the navy, and again sailed for Boston, arriving in season to take part in the battle of Bunker's Hill, having command of a division of flatboats, and acting as lieutenant of the Glasgow. On returning to his ship he was ordered to Newport, R. I., where he was appointed prizemaster of two prizes which he took safely to Boston. Soon after this he captured two American privateers that were cruising in the vicinity of Boston harbor. Having again been ordered to the Rose, this time as lieutenant, he went into the harbor of Stonington, and cut out a schooner, armed her with swivels, and proceeded with a convoy of prizes to Boston. Sailing again for Rhode Island, he fell in with an American privateer of 14 guns, and after an engagement lasting an hour and a half was obliged to withdraw, and proceeded on the way to his destination. Soon afterwards, being ordered on shore at Newport in search of deserters, he had scarcely reached the wharf when he was struck down with a cutlass, the weapon striking a button of a Dutch cap worn for disguise, which probably saved his life. Mr. Stanhope was marched to Provi-dence, and from there sent to Northampton, Mass., and lodged in prison. From here, he, with a brother soldier, George Greg-ory, made his escape, but on reaching Middletown, Conn., they were discovered and returned to Northampton, and closely watched for nine months, when he again effected an escape, this time with a Mr. Arnold. After travelling on foot some seven hund-red miles, in various disguises, he reached Salem, and after a multiplicity of trying circumstances, arrived at Halifax, Nova Scotia.

A few days previous to his capture at Newport, he had been appointed lieutenant of the Nautilus, but his first service as lieutenant after his escape was on the Milford, then on the Liv-erpool. In 1777 he reached England, and ten days after his arrival was appointed first lieutenant of the Nonesuch, and again sailed for America. After various services in Chesapeake and Delaware Bays, he once more found himself at Newport, Rhode Island. The Nonesuch being stationary, he solicited and obtained the command of the Pigott galley, and sailing close under an American battery at Bristol Ferry, was permitted to pass unmolested, and proceeded up the Swansea river, where he captured the Spitfire, repassing the battery with small loss. A second attempt proved less fortunate, as the Pigott grounded under the guns of the battery and was nearly pounded to pieces. She was soon repaired, but within a few months, and subsequent to the arrival of the French fleet, Lieut. Stanhope was under the necessity of running her on shore and blowing her to pieces. He now served on shore, and the English forces being hard pressed at Newport, he volunteered to go to headquarters for assistance. Starting out in a whaleboat, which was dragged some distance across the land from the mouth of the harbor to avoid suspicion, he proceeded on his errand. Passing under the stern of the French admiral's ship, and being hailed, he replied in French that it was the guard-boat, and was allowed to continue his course, reaching New York two days later, after encountering a severe storm which gave the lieutenant no little trouble but caused considerable damage to the French fleet. He was gladly welcomed by Lord Howe, and directed to do duty on board the Monmouth.

In 1779 he was appointed first lieutenant of the ship Portland, and was stationed off Newfoundland, where he was promoted, and became master and commander of the Trepassey. In 1781 he was sent with dispatches to the West Indies, when, on reaching the Barbadoes, he was made commander of the Salamander fire-ship, and afterwards promoted to post captain on board the Terrible of 74 guns. Subsequently he was transferred to the Russell, and was in the engagement off St. Kitts, and in 1782 returned to England with Sir William Hood's dispatches.

Captain Stanhope's next service was on board the frigate Mercury, in which he sailed for New York with the definitive treaty of peace in 1783. Before the evacuation of that post by the British troops, he proceeded in the Mercury to Nova Scotia, on the coast of which he was stationed some three years. During that time Captain Stanhope was sent to Boston, and while there claimed that certain insults or indignities were offered to himself, together with his officers and crew, and became involved in a correspondence with Gov. Bowdoin in relation to the matter.

In 1786 Captain Stanhope returned to England for the purpose of enjoying a rest after eighteen years of almost continuous service. Only a few years elapsed, however, before he was again called into service, this time as commander of the Ruby in 1794. In 1795 he sailed under orders for the Cape of Good Hope, and after its surrender returned to England with official dispatches. Subsequently he was placed in command of the Neptune of 98 guns, and later, in 1798, of the Achilles of 74 guns. He was advanced to the rank of Rear-Admiral of the Blue in 1801, and three years after to the same rank in the Red squadron. In 1805 he was appointed to command the river Thames, after the victory of Trafalgar was made Vice-Admiral of the Red, and Nov. 13, 1807, created a Baronet. He afterwards served in the expedition to the Baltic, and returning, resumed his command of the river, but in 1810 was removed to the command of the river Medway and the Nore.

Sir Edwyn Stanhope * married Peggy,† daughter of Francis Malbone, of Newport, R. I. She died Aug. 8, 1810, at Greenwich in Kent, where she was buried in a vault under the church. Their children were : Peggy, born at Newport, R. I., Jan. 6, 1785 ; Catharine, born at Maydeacon in Kent July 5, 1786 ; Ann Eliza, born at Heythe in Hampshire April 22, 1789 ; Caroline, born at Bath May 4, 1791, and died in July, 1800, at Teignmouth in Devonshire, where she was buried. Edwin Francis, born at Bath Dec. 15, 1793. Sir Edwyn Stanhope was born May 21, 1754, and died December 20, 1814.

* In the pedigree the name is given *Sir Henry Edwin*.
† Her christian name was Margaret.

On the wall above the tomb in the Church at Shelford may be found the epitaph of Sir Michael Stanhope and his wife, Anne Rawson :

Sir Michaell Stanhope Knight, whilst he lived, Governour of Hull under the late King of famous memory H. VIII. and chief Gentleman of the Privy Chamber to the late noble and good 'King Edward VI. By Sir Michaell she had Sir Thomas Stanhope of Shelford Knight. Elenor, married Thomas Cooper Esq. Edward Stanhope Esq. one of her majesties Councill in the North parts of England. Julian, married John Hotham Esq. John Stanhope Esq. one of the Gentlemen of the Privy Chamber to our most dear Sovrange Lady Queen Elizabeth. Jane married to Sir Roger Townsend. Edward Stanhope, Doctor of the Civile Law, one of her majesties high Court of Chancery. Michaell Stanhope Esq. one of the Privy Chamber to Queen Elizabeth, besides Margaret, W^m. & Edward who died in infancy. Anne Rawson the widow lived 35 years after the death of her husband & brought up her children in virtue and learning whereby they were preferred to the marriages & callings before recited in her lifetime. She kept continually a worshipful house, relieved the poor daily, gave good countenance & comfort to the preachers of Gods word, spent the most of her time in her later days in Prayer & using the church where Gods word was preached. She being old she died 20th day Feby 1587 in the 30th year of the reign aforesaid in the faith of Christ, with hope of a joyful resurrection.

In Shelford Church.

Here lyeth the body of the Lady Anne Stanhope wydowe, daughter to Nicholas Rawson of Aveley in the county of Essex, Esquier, late wife to Sir Michaell Stanhope, Knight ; which Lady Anne deceased the 20 of Febr. anno 1587. Vivit post funera virtus.

STANHOPE PEDIGREE.

Sir Richard de Stanhope (1216-1272)=

Sir Richard de Stanhope=
Lord of Estwycke, Co. of
Northumberland.
Mayor of Newcastle.

John de Stanhope=Elizabeth Maulovel
of Rampton Notts

Sir Edward Stanhope=1st, Adelina, dau. Sir Gervas Clefton.
(2d, Anna, heiress of Thos. Plantagenet)

Richard, d. s. p.

Sir Michael=Anna, dau. Nicholas Rawson.

Sir Thomas Margaret d. infancy Elenor Edward Julian Sir John, Jane Sir Michael
William " " Baron.
Edward " "

Sir John=1st, Cordell, dau. Richard Allington. Anna Thomas Edward
(He m. 2d, Catharine, dau. Thomas
Trentham. See below *)

† Sir Philip=1st, Lady Catharine, dau. Married 2d, Anne, dau. Right Hon. Sir John
Francis Lord Hastings. Pakington, K. B. For issue see page 48.

Sir Henry Lord Stanhope, K. B., from whom descended HonArthur, of
Philip Dormer Stanhope, 4th Earl, the celebrated Lord Mansfield, Wood-
Chesterfield, who d. March 24, 1773. house. M. P. Nott.
(See next page.) (See page 49.)

*Sir John of Elvaston (half-brother to Sir Philip), Knighted at Whitehall,
June 4, 1607. M. P. Died 1638. Married 1st, Olave, dau. Edward Beres-
ford; 2d, Mary, dau. Sir John Radclyffe. Sir John's grandson John had
Thomas, d. s. p.; Charles, d. s. p.; and William Stanhope, vice chamberlain
to the King, 1727, and ambassador at the Court of Spain, 1729. After concluding the treaty of Seville he was created Baron Harrington. Secretary of
State 1730 and 1744; Lord President of the Council 1742. Created Viscount
Petersham and Earl of Harrington Feb. 9, 1742; Lord Lieutenant of Ireland
1746; Lord Justice during the King's absence. Died Dec. 8, 1756.

† Knighted at Whitehall Dec. 16, 1605, and by patent dated Nov. 7, 1616;
created Lord Stanhope of Shelford, Nottinghamshire; and Aug. 4, 1628,
Earl of Chesterfield.

Sir Henry Lord Stanhope, K. B.=Catharine, dau. Thomas Lord Wotton.

(1st wife: Anne Percy.)
(2d wife: Elizabeth Butler.)
Philip=3d, Elizabeth Dormer.
2d Earl.
d. 1713.
Philip=Elizabeth Saville.
3d
Earl;
died
1726.

Philip Dormer Stanhope,
4th Earl and the celebrated Lord Chesterfield;
died March 24, 1773,
When the honors reverted to the descendants of the
Hon. Arthur Stanhope of Mansfield.

48

[See page 46.]

Hon. Alexander,=Catherine, dau. Arnold Burghill, Esq.
distinguished diplomatist; son of
Philip by 2d wife.   Became Earl
of Chesterfield.   Died 1707.

James=Lucy, dau. Thomas Pitt, Esq., of
He was a distinguished army officer; | Boconnoc, Cornwall.
was commander - in - chief of British
forces in Spain, 1708-10; as reward
for successes made principal Sec'y of
State, First Lord of the Treasury and
Chancellor of the Exchequer; Viscount
Stanhope; Baron Stanhope, 1717; Created Earl Stanhope, April 14, 1718. One
of the Lord Justices of the Kingdom.
Died Feb. 5, 1720.

Philip=Grizel, dau. Charles Lord
d. 1786 | Binning, 1745.
2d Earl |

1st, Lady Hester Pitt.*
Charles, M. P., 3d Earl=2d, Louisa, dau. Hon. Henry Gren-
Distinguished for his mechanical | ville in 1781.
genius.†   Died, 1816.

James H.‡ Charles B.§ Philip Henry=Catharine Lucy Smith.
                         4th Earl, |
                         d. 1855.

Philip Henry=Emily H. Kerrison.
5th Earl. |
Historian and biographer, d. 1875. |
Arthur Philip, 6th Earl Stanhope.

* Daughter of William Pitt, first Earl of Chatham.   She died about 1780,
leaving three daughters: Hester L., Griselda, and Lucy R.

† He was a friend of Dr. Benjamin Franklin, and through the assistance
of the Earl of Chatham, introduced him to the House of Lords, Jan. 20,
1775 (See *Our Country*, by Lossing, Vol. II., p. 760).   He remained a
staunch advocate of American liberty, and was one of the memorable major-
ity of nineteen in the House of Commons which put an end to the American
war, and to the administration of Lord North.

‡ Hon. James Hamilton, born Sept. 7, 1788; Captain and Lieut.-Col. 1st
Foot Guards; married Lady Frederica Louisa Maria Murray, dau. William,
3d Earl of Mansfield.   Their son was James Banks Stanhope of Revesby,
b. May 13, 1821, M. P. North Linc., 1851-1868.

§ Hon. Charles Banks, born 1785; Major 50th Regt., and fell at Corunna,
Jan. 16, 1809.

49

[See page 46.]

Hon. Arthur=1662, Mary or Anne, dau. of
of Mansfield | Sir Henry Salusbury, Bart.
House.

        Charlés=1674, Frances, dau. Sir Francis Topp,
           | Bart., and had five sons.

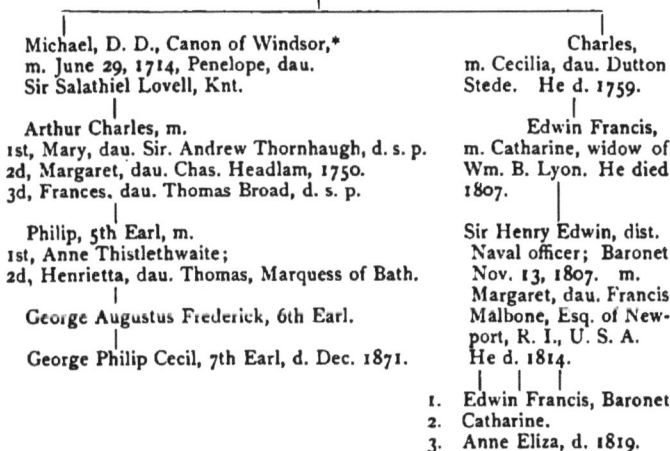

Michael, D. D., Canon of Windsor,*	Charles,
m. June 29, 1714, Penelope, dau.	m. Cecilia, dau. Dutton
Sir Salathiel Lovell, Knt.	Stede. He d. 1759.
Arthur Charles, m.	Edwin Francis,
1st, Mary, dau. Sir. Andrew Thornhaugh, d. s. p.	m. Catharine, widow of
2d, Margaret, dau. Chas. Headlam, 1750.	Wm. B. Lyon. He died
3d, Frances. dau. Thomas Broad, d. s. p.	1807.
Philip, 5th Earl, m.	Sir Henry Edwin, dist.
1st, Anne Thistlethwaite;	Naval officer; Baronet
2d, Henrietta, dau. Thomas, Marquess of Bath.	Nov. 13, 1807. m.
	Margaret, dau. Francis
George Augustus Frederick, 6th Earl.	Malbone, Esq. of New-
	port, R. I., U. S. A.
George Philip Cecil, 7th Earl, d. Dec. 1871.	He d. 1814.

                        1. Edwin Francis, Baronet
                        2. Catharine.
                        3. Anne Eliza, d. 1819.

      * Ferdinand, (son of Michael, D. D.)
      Married 1742, Mary Philips.
          |
      Admiral John, R. N.=Caroline Dent.
          |
      Charles George=Jane, dau. Sir James Galbraith.
          |
      George Philip, 8th Earl Chesterfield.

SIR JOHN RAWSON, KNIGHT OF RHODES.

As the family armorial of Sir John Rawson, Knight of Rhodes and St. John of Jerusalem, was used by the descendants of the Secretary, Edward Rawson,* after coming to Massachusetts, and as they belonged to the same family in line of descent, it may be interesting to have a more extended account of this distinguished gentleman. His father, Richard Rawson, as we have noticed on a previous page,† was elected alderman of the ward of Farringdon without London in 1475, and the following year chosen sheriff of London, and reëlected in 1478, also 1483. He was senior warden of the Mercers' Company. His wife Isabella outlived him, and, in her will dated Sept. 1, 1497, she mentions her son John Rawson, Knight of Rhodes, to whom, as well as to her other sons, Avery, Christopher, Richard and Nicholas, she gave each "one dozen silver spoons with knoppes."

This Sir John was admitted to the freedom of the Mercers' Company in 1492, and previous to A. D. 1497, possibly during a voyage to the eastern shores of the Mediterranean, had united with the order of Knights of St. John, then established at the

---

* Stacey Grimaldi, F. S. A., in his *Origines Genealogica*, says that Coats of Arms have long been considered as affording good evidence respecting families, and in continuation adds that Cromwell, Earl of Essex, had no paternal shield of arms, and in reply to some flattering heralds, who would have entitled him to the arms of the family of Cromwell of Lincolnshire, then long extinct, said he would not wear another man's coat for fear the owner thereof should pluck it off his ears; and was granted a special armorial.

Burton, the author of the History of Leicestershire, a lawyer of no mean acquirements, was so sensible of the value of these armorials, that in order to make them still more useful to posterity, collected copies of them from stained glass windows, monuments, and other sources, for the avowed purpose that they might rectify armories and genealogies, and give such testimony and proof as might put an end to many differences.

† See page 8.

Island of Rhodes. He was appointed Prior of Kilmainham in 1511, and by the command of King Henry VIII. made one of the Privy Councillors of Ireland, Lord Treasurer of that kingdom, and a member of the Irish house of peers. March 6, 1522, he was constrained from going to the Island of Rhodes to assist in its defence from the attacks of the Turks by Cardinal Wolsey, who felt the importance of his remaining in Ireland. But the extreme danger to which the order of St. John of Jerusalem was exposed at Rhodes, through the impending attack by the Turkish arms under Solyman the magnificent, and the imperative summons issued by the Grand Master calling on all the Knights in every land to rally at once to his aid, compelled Sir John Rawson to proceed immediately to the Island, where he was assigned a place at the head of the English-speaking Knights, and was no doubt present and took part in that memorable and heroic defence of Rhodes in the year 1522, when six hundred Knights, with a limited number of military retainers, held two hundred thousand Turks at bay for six months, and until the Knights obtained an honorable capitulation, although they were forced to abandon the Island. As early as July 28, 1524, Sir John had returned to Ireland. A. D. 1525 the Grand Master of the Knights visited England and was well received by King Henry VIII., who desired the Grand Master to confer the Grand Priory of Ireland upon the Turcopilier, Brother John Rawson by name, who had been very serviceable to him in the government of the Island, and whose gentle administration had been instrumental in polishing and civilizing its inhabitants. The Grand Master in order to show his complacence to the King, engaged John Babington, about A. D. 1527, to resign the Priory of Ireland to Rawson, who by way of exchange made a resignation to him of the Priory of Dinemor and the dignity of Turcopilier. The Grand Master also caused it to be arranged, that if Babington should come to be Grand Prior of England, he should pay Rawson a pension of 1800 livres. All this so pleased the King that he confirmed all the orders, and sent the Grand Master a bason and cup of massive gold set with precious stones. The office of

Turcopilier was one of great dignity in the order ; he was conventual bailiff, commander of the cavalry of the order, and of the guards stationed at the court, the most important office of the order in the English tongue.

Sir John again went to the aid of the Grand Master, at this time in Italy, being there June 3, 1527, while yet holding the office of Prior of Ireland. In October, 1528, the King sent him into Ireland with important dispatches to the Earl of Ossory, who was then engaged in invading the country of the Earl of Desmond, and during that visit the Lord-Deputy of Ireland was entertained by the Priors of Kilmainham, Christchurch and All Saints with an exhibition at Christchurch of stage plays on Scripture subjects. Rawson immediately returned to England on special business, he then being under-treasurer of Ireland ; from 1530 to July, 1532, he was Lord Treasurer of that kingdom. In 1538, while on one of his visiting tours, he was taken sick with the palsy, and being unable to travel, he, August 7, wrote to the King from St. Davids, Wales, stating the condition of matters in Ireland, mentioning the serious hardships his English subjects were being exposed to by the enemies of the King. Sir John sent this letter forward at the hand of his brother Richard, the Archdeacon of Essex and Canon of Windsor, who he writes had been with him during the past six months. From 1535 to 1542 he was again actively engaged in performing his official duties in Ireland, being present at the yielding of the Castle of Old Rosse by Cahir McCarthy, and addressed a letter to the King from the "Camp of your hoste." The following month he was recommended by Brabazon to be Chancellor of Ireland.

November 6, 1538, the Archbishop brought a specific charge against the Prior of Kilmainham ; it was for keeping a servant of the Archbishop nineteen weeks in the castle at Dublin. Notwithstanding the fact that the charge came from such high authority there were several prominent and distinguished gentlemen ready to address the King in behalf of Sir John Rawson, among them Sir Anthony St. Leger, Lord Deputy of Ireland. September 12, 1540 the King acceded to the recommendations of the

Lord Deputy, and the case was arranged, Sir John surrendering the office of Prior of Kilmainham, and receiving instead five hundred marks per annum out of the estate of the hospital during the remainder of his life. A. D. 1541 he was created Viscount Clontarff, with a pension of ten pounds per annum for life. Dec. 7, 1542 the Lord Deputy and Council addressed the King, stating that Sir John Rawson while Lord Treasurer, had disbursed the sum of one hundred and seventy-three pounds eleven shillings and four pence above his receipts, and now that his health was poor, and he was not well able to care for himself as formerly, asked that the money be made up to him in part at least, and and that Sir John was willing and would be content to take his own account as kept by himself, which was thirty-two pounds less than the amount shown by the present treasurer's books as being due him, as he was at that time sick. We presume he recovered the money, as he seems to have been held in good favor by the King. He also recovered his health, for he survived until the year 1560.

This Sir John Rawson seems to have been the most distinguished person bearing the family name within the range of our careful research. His brothers Avery, Christopher, Richard and Nicholas, were each of them also quite prominent for their time, two of them as ministers, and the other two as merchants in London. The writer has received within a few months, through the kindness of Judge Hamilton B. Staples of Worcester, Mass., a photograph of a brass plate which, during one of his recent trips across the water, he found inlaid in a marble slab lying in one of the aisles of that historic old church in London known as Allhallows, or All Saints Barking Church, situated on Barking Alley, near the east end of Great Tower street. The photograph was obtained from a copy made of the tablet. The brass plate has on it three figures nine inches in height, representing Christopher Rawson, the merchant of London, and his two wives, Margaret and Agnes, standing on a base bearing the following inscription : "—of Christopher Rawson, late mercer of London, merchant of the staple of Calais, which deceased the Second day

of October an° Dom. 9 Henry VIII., 1518, and Margaret and
Agnes, his wives, which Agnes died the — day of —— anno Dm
1500 ——."

The first part of the original inscription as well as the latter
portion have been erased ; whether it was done in Cromwell's
time for obliterating from the church all connections with the
church of Rome, to which the inscription may have referred, I
know not, although that may have been the case. Each of the
figures are represented as standing erect, wearing long robes,
with the palms of their hands brought together at the breast in
the attitude of prayer. Over the head of each figure is a scroll
on which are some characters not fully discernible.

On page 8, in referring to this Christopher Rawson, the writer
stated that his wife Margaret was the mother of his children. It
will be seen by the pedigree that it was Agnes and not Margaret.

ADDENDA 1972

WHEN ON DECEMBER 29, 1940, All Hallows by the Tower
was burnt out by incendiary bombs (having been hit
by high explosives, above the High Altar, three weeks
before) and the walls became a glowing fence enclosing hot
stones and molten lead, these Brasses lay beneath. Three
were recovered in the process of restoring the North Aisle.
The others remained beneath the rubble of destruction and
a protecting layer of asphalt until 1951. The full restoration
of the Church then began, and as the contractors' men
lifted the asphalt carpet and started to remove the rubble,
there followed them (almost step by step) the Verger,
Comd. Gunner C. W. Tisshaw, R.N. (retd.). His energy
and vigilance were fully rewarded, for he recovered all the
other brasses, as he had done the first three.

Christopher Rawson, 1518

This has three figures over an inscription in English. The centre figure of Christopher Rawson is placed between those of his two wives, Margaret and Agnes. At the top of the brass is a scroll inscribed in Latin "*O Beata Trinitas*", and proceeding from the mouths of the figures are other scrolls with "*Libera Nos*", "*Justifica Nos*" and "*Salva Nos*", respectively. It is interesting to note the reference to Justification. At this time the controversy in regard to justification by Faith or Works was in full swing.

Christopher Rawson was the son of Richard Rawson and Isabella (Crawford), who owned the old Wool Quay and left it to her son. His Will dated 30th September, 1518 gives precise instructions as to the lay-out and pattern of his tomb, and directs his burial in the Chapel of Our Blessed Lady set on the South Side of the Parish Church.

ALL HALLOWS by the TOWER, LONDON

Visitors to the Tower of London often are not aware that close by just across the street from the Tower Entrance is a very old church. All Hallows Berkyngechirche was once a dependency of the famous Abbey of Barking in Essex. The church was founded about A.D. 640 and 680. In this church were held trials for blasphemy and heresy by papal inquisitors, especially concerning the Knights Templars. On Sept. 2, 1666 Pepys recorded in his diary how he went ''up to the top of Barking Steeple'' and watched ''the great fires, oyle-cellars and brimstone and other things burning'' until he ''became afeared to stay there long and down again as fast as I could.'' Barking Church escaped the fate of so many London churches on that day.

St Mullen

S.Androm

S.Mington ínber eaft

Mbullians Rerling

Thisker

Lion Kay

Billinsgate

Bridge Gate

BRIDGE

rke

lay Oueris

In 1966 my wife and I found the 'bombed out' church-All Hallows-beautifully reconstructed with much of the original walls and floors intact. We were unable to find the Christopher Rawson brass memorial. Several years later during a visit to London my niece, Miss Eunice Rawson of Bristol, Wis., and my sister, Mrs. Roma Rawson Herrick of Harvard, Ill. not only found the brass memorial but took a photograph and secured copies of brass rubbings. The Vicar Sidney E. Hughes was most helpful and showed them the ancient volume in which is recorded the directions for burial in the church requested by Christopher. Members of the Rawson family who visit this church and who indicate to the Vicar that they are descendents of Christopher will find a very cooperative church staff. Also, the site of the Old Wool Quay which Christopher inherited from his mother is only a short distance westerly on Lower Thames Street close to the Billingsgate Market. Yes, it smells like fish.

COLNBROOK See pages 9, 27 and 28. The Secretary's grandfather owned considerable property in Colnbrook including a house, The Draggon, and several other buildings used for his business. His own father, David, was born and grew up here. Since David died rather young, the boy Edward probably spent some time here in this village.

Colnbrook is located on the old road from London to Bath approximately seventeen miles west of London — the mile post in the village so states. Since it was a great thoroughfare and coaching town it contained many inns, some of which have come down through the years in good repair. ''The Ostrich'' is the oldest inn on the 'Road to Bath' and is the fourth oldest inn in England. The English novelist, Thomas Delany, a contemporary of Shakespeare, wrote a novel based on happenings at this inn. Briefly, many murders were committed in this inn by the landlord and his wife. Using a spy hole to make sure that the intended victim was asleep, a hinged trap door was sprung which debouched the sleeper into the brew house below and into the boiling liquid in the vat. Supposedly sixty murders were thus executed. Should you visit Colnbrook, you may have your meals amid very historical surroundings, or if you wish to forget murders, the St. George Inn is nearly as old.

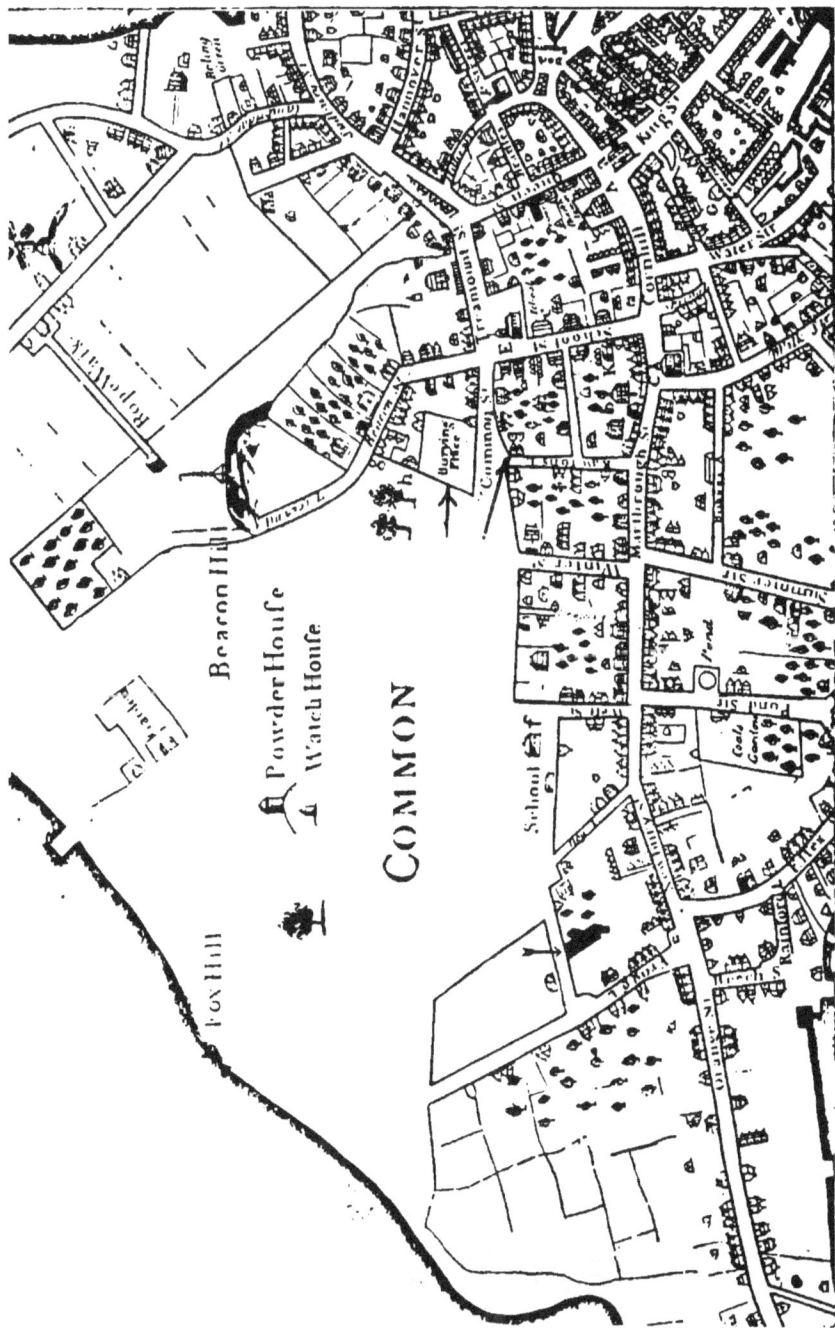

Beacon Hill

♟ Powder House
♟ Watch House

COMMON

Fox Hill

Ropewalk

Burying Place

Common Str

Hanover

King Str

Water Str

Cornhill

School

Marlborough

Summer Str

Pond

Pond Str

Coals Garden

School Str

From Bonner's Map of Boston, 1722

COLNBROOK

BOUNDARY BRIDGE AND BRIDGE STREET

This quiet, clean, and attractive village gives little indication of the frightful bombings it received during W.W. II. One of the largest Hurricane Aircraft factories in England was located two miles westerly in Slough, and in case the bombs missed Slough, Colnbrook was handy.

With the help of Headmaster Clarke of the local school system we attempted to find the site of the Rawson owned house, The Draggon. This seems to be one of the inns or houses which were torn down many years ago.

Bus transportation from London to Colnbrook is easy and excellent.

PEDIGREE CHART   On page 33 will be found a footnote in which Mr. Crane indicates his disappointment in not being able to complete the Rawson Pedigree Chart free of missing links and doubts. In 1939 I visited Mr. William Dodge in Sutton, Mass., he being a son of Reuben Rawson Dodge who did so much to make the Rawson Memoirs possible. At that time he gave me his copy of ''The Ancestry of Edward Rawson'' which has been used in this re-printing. He asked me to turn to page 33 and showed me where he had drawn a line between John Rawson and Edward-Bridget Warde, saying that he was certain that this relationship had been verified. I am corresponding with two Christopher Rawsons in London and hope to confirm this further.

TO NEWBURY-MASSACHUSETTES BAY COLONY. In 1637 young Edward Rawson and his new bride sailed for Newbury. While some authors have produced fiction dealing with early Atlantic voyages, one of the best descriptions of making an Atlantic crossing in those years was written by Governor John Winthrop, ''History of New England'' 1630-1649.

RACHEL PERNE: Much more has been written about Edward Rawson and his ancestry than about the background of his young wife, Rachel Perne of Gillingham, Dorsetshire. The following information has been furnished by Mr. Asa R. Taylor, 14915 Whitfield Ave., Pacific Palisades, Cal.

RACHEL PERNE, married Edward Rawson. Rachel Perne, from ''Your Family Tree'' by David Starr Jordon, Ph.D., LL.D. Chancellor Emeritus of Leland Stanford University, and Sarah Louisa Kimball, 1929 on Page 159.

Upper: Edward Rawson Plantation House, High St.
Newburyport, Mass.

Bottom: Fireplace in the Rawson Home

DAVID I, KING OF SCOTLAND, m. Maud, daughter of Waldeophus, Earl of Northumberland.

Henry, Prince of Scotland, Earl of Huntington, m. Ada (or Adeline), daughter of William de Warren, Earl of Warren, 2nd Earl of Surrey, and his wife, Isabel de Vermandois.

David, Earl of Huntington, crusader (brother of Malcolm IV and William IV, the Lion, Kings of Scotland), m. Maud de Meschines, daughter of Hugh Kyveliock, 5th Earl Palatine of Chester.

Margaret, eldest daughter (sister of Isabel, M. Robert Bruce, ancestor of King Robert Bruce), m. Alan McDonal, Lord of Galloway, Constable of Scotland.

Helen McDonal, m. Roger de Quincey, 2nd Earl of Winchester, crusader, son of Saire de Quincey, Earl of Winchester, a Magna Charta surety.

Elene De Quincey, m. Sir Alan, Lord Zouche of Ashby.

Eudo De Zouche, m. Millicent de Cantilupe.

Lucy De Zouche, m. Thomas de Greene.

Sir Henry De Greene, Lore Chief Justice of England, 1353; m. Catherine de Drayton, also of royal descent.

Sir Henry De Greene, beheaded; m. Matilda de Mauduit, and had Thomas De Greene, third son, of Green's Norton, grandfather of John De Greeme, the fugitive, father of Robert Greene, of Gillingham, Dorset, father of Richard Greene, of Bowridge Hall, Gillingham, m. Mary Hooker, and had Peter, Richard, Robert, John (a surgeon at Salisbury, came to Warwick, R.I.) and

Rachel Greene, who married Richard Perne, of Gillingham, and had Rachel Perne, who married Edward Rawson, 1615-1693, who came to Newbury, afterward to Boston, Massachusetts, and was Secretary of the Massachusetts Bay Colony 1650-81.

The Tafts of Ohio are descended from Edward and Rachel (Perne) Rawson in the following manner: Rev. Edward Grindal Rawson, Edmund Rawson, Abner Rawson, Rhoda Rawson and Aaron Taft, Peter Rawson Taft and Sylvia Howard, Alphonso Taft and Maria Torry, also of royal descent and William Howard Taft.

EDWARD RAWSON IN NEWBURY: A metal roadside historical marker on High Street in Newburyport reads: "EDWARD RAWSON, ON THIS SITE DWELT EDWARD RAWSON, SECRETARY OF THE BAY COLONY FOR THIRTY-SIX YEARS, DEPUTY TO THE GENERAL COURT FOR TWELVE YEARS, ELECTED CLERK OF THE HOUSE OF DEPUTIES IN 1646. HE DIED IN BOSTON 1693.

E.R. came to Newbury as a very young man. He was listed early as one of the most wealthy of the grantees with the number of acres in their holdings affixed to their names.

Mr. Richard Dummer 1080
Mr. Henry Sewall 630
Mr. Edward Rawson 581
Mr. John Clark 540
Mr. John Woodbridge 237
Mr. John Cutting 220
Mr. James Noyes 124
Capt. B. Greenleaf 122

Wealth determined, right or wrong, the right to vote, the amount of lace permitted on the clothing of the family, and the seating in the church.

He soon erected the "Plantation House" on his holdings. He sold this to Mr. William Pilsbury on Dec. 13, 1651 and it has remained in the Pilsbury family until the fall of 1971 when it was purchased by Mrs. James G. Zafris Jr., 264 High St., Newburyport Mass. 01950. In the last 50 years changes have been made in this home which, of course, did not increase the historical value. We understand that the new owner is concerned about restoring the building to something closer to its original form.

The American Poet, John Greenleaf Whittier, lived at Amesbury, three miles from Newburyport for 56 years. Van Wyck Brooks in his "Flowering of New England" has this to say about him: "Whittier's longest prose-piece, Margaret Smith's Journal, was a picture of the New England settlements in the days of the Salem witches. In a semi-archaic style, composed in tone and only less intense than Hawthorne's pictures, it conveyed a state of mind of the Pilgrim settlers with a haunting particularity."

Whittier based this volume on the story of the Edward Rawson family. His description of travel from Boston to Newbury, of life at 'Uncle Rawson's' and of church and governmental matters is very helpful in understanding life in the early days. Long out of print this volume may be had at a few historical libraries.

ADDITIONAL COPIES of this reprint may be had at $2.00 postpaid by writing Mr. K. O. Rawson, 49 Twentieth St., Clintonville, Wis. 54929.

www.ingramcontent.com/pod-product-compliance
Lightning Source LLC
Chambersburg PA
CBHW021628270326
41931CB00008B/929